Searching

for

Success

Billy Arcement, M.Ed.

Results Press
Donaldsonville, LA

Library of Congress Number: LC 96-094443

ISBN: 0-9653446-0-6

Acknowledgments

With special thanks to:

Monica Crews and Louise McLaughlin for their outstanding editing and many suggestions to improve the meaning of words.

Joe Bonura, CSP, fellow speaker and friend, the first person to buy this book (sight unseen and unwritten). Thank you for your encouragement and confidence that I could complete this project.

Jack Canfield, CSP, co-author of the best seller *Chicken Soup for the Soul,* for taking time to talk to me about writing a book. Your wisdom was the breakthrough experience that moved this project to closure.

Melessa Gonsoulin, whose talents and artistry created the book cover design.

My wife, Ernestine, for the love and belief that keeps me going.

My children, their spouses, and my grandchildren who continue to bring joy and happiness to my life.

Contents

Part I: Discover Your Purpose

Living With Yourself   17
The Most Valuable And Essential Things In Life   22
Building Your Dreams   26

Part II: Develop The Right Attitude

How Did The Pot Get Black?   39
If Only   41
One Man's Junk Is Another Man's Treasure   44
The Desire To Improve Yourself   47
Your Self-concept And Success   49
Some Guiding Principles   51

Part III: Develop A Career, Not A Job

Going The Extra Mile   59
Implementing Change In A Positive Way   62
Some Thoughts About Work   67
You're A Boss In Trouble If You...   71
The Secret To Getting Promoted   73
How To Find And Keep A Job   77

Part IV: Two Important Keys To Success— Discipline And Persistence

Power 87
Self-Competition 90
The Invisible Barriers 93
Adding Years To Life 95
Just One More Time 98

Part V: School Is Never Out

Pretend You're The IRS 107
The Reading Habit 109
Learning From Others 112
Finding Yourself 115

Part VI: Develop A Daily Structure

A Good Way To Start The Day 123
Moments Of Life 127

Part VII: Build People Bridges

The Golden Gift 141
You Only Pass Through Once 143
Getting People To Like You 146
We Are All In The Customer Service Business 149
Make Me A Part Of Your World 152

Part VIII: Success Challenges

Don't Just Be—Become!   163
It's All In Our Point Of View   165
I Dare You   167
Learning To Decide   170
The Forgotten Law Of Life   173

Part IX: Closing Thoughts

The Manresa Experience   181
The Manresa Prayer   184
Three Wishes For You   186

Part X: Lagniappe

Reading List   193
About The Author   197

▮▮
Introduction

Throughout our lives, we are on a hunt. We search for the magical keys that will unlock the doors of success. The identity of those keys is not the same for everyone.

Some see success as the accumulation of money and material goods. Some find their success in the development of strong family ties. Others use the development of a satisfying career as the measuring stick for success. What about you? How do you measure success? Where do you concentrate your search? What is your ultimate destination?

As I began to develop ideas for this book, I sought my own focus in the success arena. No matter where my thoughts ventured, I kept coming back to one idea. And that idea eventually became the core for each chapter.

This one idea is so powerful yet so obvious that many never grasp its significance. Not understanding this idea is the root for most personal failures in life. What is this powerful idea that is so influential to personal success? It is the idea of **accepting full responsibility for our successes.**

When we fully realize that no one is coming to the rescue, we open the doors for growth. When we continue to believe that our faith is controlled by outside forces, we close the doors of opportunity. If I accomplish no other goal with this book than to wake you to the realization that you are in charge of your life, I've reached my success goal.

As you read through each chapter, do so at a speed that will provide opportunities to think and absorb the thoughts shared. At the end of each of the nine parts there is an action list and a place to write your ideas. Take advantage of these exercises. They provide extra value to you.

At the end of the book I've provided you with a list of books I have found especially beneficial in my personal search for success. As an action step, begin to acquire these books, reading them with the same care I'm advocating for this book.

The idea to write a book had its beginnings about fifteen years ago. At that time, I was broadcasting a weekly motivational program, *"Take Charge of Your Life,"* on a local radio station. Over the years since initially producing these weekly scripts, I gave some thought to using them for a book. I also went through a number of other ideas. None seemed to jell and no matter how hard I tried, I just couldn't put it all together to complete the project. It appeared overwhelming—I was stuck in first gear.

In January 1995, I made a commitment to have the first draft completed before the end of the year. It was time to put up or shut up. I started writing but by mid-year, I hadn't made much progress. Time was getting short. Frustrated but determined, I went to the National Speakers Association (NSA) annual convention in July looking for an answer to help me complete the project.

As I looked through the convention program, I noticed that Mark Victor Hanson, CSP and Jack Canfield, CSP, co-authors of the best seller, *Chicken Soup for the Soul,* were doing a session on how they wrote and published their book. That session was the stimulus I needed. I left their session eager to begin writing. Subsequent conversation with Jack Canfield provided even more insights. By now I was really excited.

In the hall, I met fellow speaker and friend, Joe Bonura, CSP. We talked about my book. Joe gave me a twenty dollar bill for the first copy. Now it was impossible to back down. I had sold a book!

I returned home, framed Joe's twenty and placed it next to my computer. I can't explain what happened next. It was almost magical. Words began to pour out of my head almost faster than I could write them. Before long, I had sixty pages written. I couldn't believe what was happening. There were weak moments but, December 29 at 11:30 p.m., I completed the draft, *two days ahead of schedule!*

Much of what I wrote got revised in the editing but the final product is a much stronger and meaningful document. That's what good editing does for you. I'm proud of the finished product. Giving "birth" to the book was worth all the labor pains I experienced. The process was so enjoyable that two more books have been conceptualized and are growing to maturity. Plans are to deliver a second one next year. I think Jack, Mark, and Joe started a population explosion!

Thank you for reading this creation. I pray that you will find the messages stimulating and informative. I wish you well as you journey on your search for success.

Billy Arcement

Part I

Discover Your Purpose

Key Points:

1. Use your talents and potential.
2. Don't blame others.
3. Accept full responsibility for your life.
4. Set out on the path of positive change.
5. It is never too late to use talents.
6. Questions help assess talents.
7. We think and take action on our thoughts.
8. We only get results from action.
9. We have a free will and the power to choose.
10. Develop a personal strategic plan.
11. Learn strengths and weaknesses.
12. Write goals.
13. Periodically evaluate your position.
14. Practice visualization.
15. Prioritize goals.

Each one of us is in this world to fulfill a purpose. Our charge is to act on that purpose and to use our talents to bring this purpose into reality. It is these actions that tell the world who we are.

Living With Yourself

Cavett Robert, founder of the National Speakers Association and a great motivational speaker in his own right, tells this story. A father observed his young daughter putting sugar into her tea. After the seventh teaspoon, he could no longer restrain himself. "Darling," he said as he grabbed her hand, "Don't you think that will make your tea too sweet?" "No Daddy," she replied innocently, "Not if I don't stir it!"

There's a great lesson in this amusing story. Like the young girl, many go through life never stirring their tea of talents and abilities. They have great potential but never put it to use. This loss is one of the greatest tragedies of life.

I truly believe that everyone is on this earth for a purpose. All of us have a role to play in the divine scheme of things. Our responsibility is to look deeply into ourselves to find our purpose. We are all charged to make a contribution but, strangely enough, not forced to do so. That remains our choice. We have that freedom!

I don't believe anyone ever sets out to fail. People seldom fail because they don't have the ability to succeed. Rather, failure comes because too much of the power we possess remains dormant. We barely mine the vein of pure gold we possess—our God-given talents and abilities.

Why is this so? I believe the answer is so simple that the logic escapes most people. When things go wrong, our first tendency is to fix blame rather than accept responsibility for the failure. Think about the last time you experienced a major setback. What was your first reaction? If you honestly assess that reaction, odds are that you first looked outside yourself for the blame. That's normal. It's always easier to blame something other than ourselves. Squarely facing the reality of a bad situation takes courage and a strong willingness to grow.

What would have happened to Helen Keller had she chosen to make excuses for her blindness and deafness? She would have come and gone and the world would have lost the tremendous influence she made on the lives of millions.

What would have happened if a young girl, hardly able to walk, had given up and accepted the future of being crippled? World class runner Wilma Rudolph would not make excuses. She worked and worked until she became the best runner of her time. Both women had the opportunity to give up but neither chose to make excuses for the deficiencies life brought them. They decided to concentrate on their gifts and ignore their shortcomings.

Life's greatest gift comes in the form of the abundance of natural talents we possess. What are your gifts? Do you sing, talk, or write better than most? Have you special talents with wood? Can you sew or cook well? Are you a good problem solver? Are you gifted athletically? How's your dancing ability? Do you write poetry, draw, or paint well?

It's never too late! Grandma Moses was in her eighties before the world recognized her painting abilities. Colonel Sanders was retired on social security when he began his journey to build the Kentucky Fried Chicken chain of fast food restaurants.

My goal is to awaken that sleeping giant within you and help you realize that you are in charge of your life. When things are going well, we gladly accept responsibility for the success. But we must be equally willing to accept responsibility when things go wrong. This is the ultimate "take charge" act.

To be truly successful, *we must learn how to move from fixing blame to accepting full responsibility for our lives.* Reaching this pinnacle is a sign of true maturity.

Throughout this book I share ideas to help you learn how to accept responsibility. Full acceptance will set you free! Full acceptance is the essence of learning how to live with yourself. If you're unhappy with your present position in life, the place to start is with you. Once you get yourself right, your world becomes right. It's only in seeking that you will find. It's only in doing that you achieve.

American author Thomas Wolfe said, *"If a man has talent and cannot use it, he has failed. If he has talent and uses only half of it, he has partly failed. If he has talent and learns to use the whole of it, he has succeeded and won satisfaction and triumph few men ever know."*

Now is the time to change and begin to tap all the unused resources within yourself. Begin today to make your life what it is capable of becoming. You have much more ability than you think you have. You only need to look deeply within yourself to find it.

One way to begin this journey into self-discovery is to use the questioning technique. I will pose many questions throughout this book. To maximize your learning experience, take the time to think deeply and answer every question. Add your own questions in the margin. Proper use of the questioning technique can be life-changing. It's a key step toward learning personal responsibility.

My initial question is, *"Are you willing to start the journey toward positive change?"*

Living with yourself requires learning more about yourself every day. As you learn, you must make the necessary changes required to propel you forward and maximize your achievements. And that brings me to the second important point in this chapter—**you must take action on the knowledge you gain.** Knowledge without action is no different from having no knowledge at all. *No action, no change!*

Here are some questions that will help you gain knowledge about yourself. Carefully think about each answer and develop an action plan for each one.

1. *Who am I?*
2. *What are my greatest strengths?*
3. *What are my greatest weaknesses?*
4. *What talents, when used, provide the greatest joy in my life?*
5. *What do I like to do?*
6. *What don't I like to do?*
7. *What talents have helped me succeed at activities I've undertaken?*
8. *What do I like about myself?*
9. *What don't I like about myself?*
10. *What talents, when properly used, make a difference in the lives of the people I love and associate with on a day-to-day basis?*
11. *What talents could I use to increase my productivity on the job and help advance my career?*
12. *What commitments to improve am I willing to make after answering the previous questions?*

I don't promise that the journey will be easy. These are

penetrating questions that require a very open dialogue to answer. Tap your mind. It is like the waters of Niagara Falls, powerful, abundant, and flowing with force. Use the answers to make a difference in your life and in the lives of everyone you meet.

I trust you are ready because you've picked up this book. *"I am responsible,"* is a serious statement. I wish you well as you move through your journey of self-discovery and your search for success.

The power to choose, like our ability to think, is a unique gift.

The Most Valuable And Essential Things In Life

In the previous chapter, I stressed the importance of finding our purpose and maximizing our talents. Here I want to expand those ideas and tie them to four free gifts given to us by our Creator. Combined, they are powerful tools that can help make our search clearer and more focused.

No one is born neutral. We all come into the world with enough basic wiring to conduct a current. Whatever charge we make on the world depends upon how well we tap our own natural resources. My belief is that we all have sufficient skills and talents to do what we truly desire to do with our life. Notice that I didn't say "wish to do." I said, "truly desire."

During her youth, Marie Bacala was struck with rheumatic fever. After she married, she wanted to have a child. She was warned by her doctor that childbirth would shorten her life. The rheumatic fever had damaged her heart. Bearing a child would only intensify that damage. But Marie had a desire that even the risk of death could not diminish. She pursued her dream and gave birth to a beautiful girl. Eleven years later, Marie died.

Marie's desire is the ultimate example of pursuing your dream. Fortunately, most of us won't have to face such a life-threatening event to fulfill our deepest desire.

I am saddened by Marie's early death and admire her courage, determination, capacity to love, and willingness to sacrifice. That daughter she brought into the world became my wife. Without Marie's strong desire to be a mother, I would not have met my wife and our four children would never have been born.

Marie understood at an early age what her ultimate desire was. What about you? Have you identified your deepest desire? Have you determined your life's purpose? What do you want the world to remember about your time here? What difference do you want to make?

These tough questions demand much thought to get meaningful answers. The strength of the answers depends directly on how well you use your pool of talents and skills. Here are four valuable and essential things we bring to life that help maximize these natural skills:

1. *Our ability to think.* No other living organism has the brain power we possess. No other living organism can think at our level. This trait alone places humans at the apex of life's triangle. However, most people are reluctant to practice this skill. They want everyone else to think for them. They just want to do and not to think. Experts say we tap only a small percentage of our brain power—three to five percent. Yet, with only this small portion of our brain, all inventions and innovations of humanity have evolved. Imagine what we could do by just doubling our use!

2. *Our ability to take action on our thoughts.* Step one is important. But if we do nothing with the knowledge gained by thinking, it's no different from not thinking at all. We must take action. We cannot keep our car of accomplishments in neutral. We must put it in drive to move forward and reach a destination. Now is the time to begin. Take action and watch what happens.

3. *Our ability to get results from our action.* My mission as a speaker is to help my audience turn knowledge into results. By focusing our thinking and planning on steps that can produce the results we desire, we can more quickly accomplish our dreams. You should take a similar approach. Make it your mission to always maximize your talents and the choice of actions fueled by these talents. When you practice perfectly, you get perfect results.

4. *Our free will.* The power to choose, like our ability to think, is a unique gift. We don't have to rely on instinct like other animals. We can think and thus make choices. This wonderful ability is given to us free of charge. We should constantly remind ourselves that no matter how desperate our circumstances, we always have the ability to influence our destiny through the choices we make. By learning to make the right choices, we will reap the rewards we seek. That's the way it works.

The key is to always be able to remind ourselves that we are in charge. We control our destiny. Victor Frankl, in his great classic, *Man's Search For Meaning,* wrote about his experiences in the World War II Nazi concentration camps. One might think there was very little choice in this environment. But the one thing that couldn't be stopped was the power of the mind. No matter what physical tortures Frankl endured, his captors couldn't stop his thinking. He made the choice to choose his attitude no matter the circumstance. He chose his own way. To that decision, he credits his survival mentally and physically.

You may be in your own concentration camp right now. But, like Frankl, you have a choice. You have the choice to succumb or survive. You have the choice to give up or get up. What will you do?

Spend time thinking and formulating goals you truly desire to achieve Make detailed action steps for the achievement of those goals. Don't quit until you reach your destination. And, along the way, always remember that you have a free will and can make choices to adjust the journey and guarantee success.

26

Becoming the best you can possibly be won't happen by accident. Successful living demands a plan.

Building Your Dreams

My favorite month of the year is January. For someone who hates winter, this is a bold statement. Why do I like January even though I hate the cold? This is the time of the year when I develop goals for the year. I use January as my annual rejuvenation period. I spend time giving thanks for what I've managed to accomplish and forgiving myself for all the things I didn't do. For me, it is a refreshing experience to start over.

Much has been written about setting resolutions at the beginning of the new year. The central theme of such stories seems to be many promises, few deliveries. In this chapter, I want to share techniques that work. Follow these steps and January may become your favorite month as well.

The term I like to use for this process is personal strategic planning. In reality, it is the development of a strategic plan designed to move you from where you are to where you want to be. It is personal because it is a plan specific to you. It is an easy process to develop. To help, I've provided the following steps to build your plan.

1. *Take a personal inventory.* Each year, companies take inventory of their stock. I believe it's a good idea for people to do the same thing with their lives. Begin the process by taking a piece of paper and dividing it into two columns. Label one column strengths (usually the things you like to do) and the other weaknesses (usually the things you don't like to do). Don't overlook anything. It's gut-checking time.

The normal tendency people have is to list more weaknesses than strengths. Don't succumb to this tendency. Search deeply in an open and honest fashion. The more information you can write, the more you can learn. Complete this step in a relaxing environment. Don't rush. This is a time for deep thoughts and thorough investigations. If you truly trust and value the opinion of someone, you might ask them to contribute to the list. This can be a risk but it can also reveal blind spots we don't know exist. Another option is to develop the list and have your friend review it and provide feedback.

2. *Develop a goal list.* Without concern for how you will do it, start writing all the things you would like to do. Consider goals that involve physical, spiritual, emotional, mental, social, and financial areas of your life. Dream big. There are no limitations. Carry the list with you and, as you think of something, jot it down. Continue this process over several days. Strive to reach 100 goals or more. Remember, there are no limitations.

In a recent series of programs I was conducting for a client, I asked participants to write 100 goals. At the following session, a young man remarked that he could only come up with twelve items, and all of them were goals he had thought about achieving after he completed high school. I asked how long ago that was. He replied, "Ten years." Then he quickly added, "I've just realized that I've wasted ten years of my life."

The exercise made him take a serious look at his life and the accomplishments he had achieved. It was a brutal awakening but hopefully the start of a new direction. If your direction is unclear, this exercise could turn out to be your wake-up call.

3. *Prioritize the goal list.* Take your goal list and begin to focus on the items that are really important to you at this time. As you rethink your list, some items will drop off. That's okay.

Give each goal a desire test. Find those items that build excitement within you even when you read them. Rate each item on a scale of one through ten with ten representing the highest score. The goals with the highest scores represent your highest priorities and are the goals you start working first.

Besides desire, you must have an unwavering belief that you can reach the goal. Lacking belief is a sure way to guarantee failure. Using the desire/belief criteria to prioritize will assure you that you are working on the right priorities.

4. *Refine the language of your goal so that it is specific, sufficiently detailed to be clearly defined, measurable, and challenging.* Once you've done this step, place a deadline next to the goal. Say exactly when you plan to complete all action steps and bring the goal into reality. Be realistic, but firm with yourself.

Here is an example of how a college freshman, beginning school in September 1996, might write a goal about completing her college education.

"I will complete my degree in biology, with a minor in chemistry, by June 1, 2000." That goal is specific, clearly defined, measurable, and certainly challenging.

5. *Check for balance.* Review the final list to be sure the goals reflect activities that cover your physical, spiritual, social, mental, emotional (personal growth), and financial desires. One area might need shoring up but don't just work on that area at the expense of all the others. A multidimensional approach is best.

6. *Give yourself some reasons to complete the goals.* What will you gain if you complete a goal? What benefits do you derive? Those are important questions to consider as you choose a goal. If you gain nothing of value, why take the time to work on a goal? Listing benefits also provides incentives for completion. Do this for each goal you've chosen.

7. *Determine the information you will need to complete your goals.* We are not automatically prepared to achieve a goal just because we desire it. Some goals require that we go back to school or educate ourselves in some way before they are achievable. Be prepared to do what you must do to reach your destination.

8. *Identify obstacles in your way.* Besides education, there may be other obstacles preventing the successful accomplishment of a goal. These issues must be identified early in the process so the necessary steps can be taken to maintain progress.

9. *Seek help when you need it.* Some of your goals require the aid of individuals or organizations. For each goal, make a list of sources you can use to help and how you plan to solicit that help.

10. *Build your action steps.* After you've written the goals and taken care of all the previously discussed information, it's time to get down to serious business. For each goal, develop a detailed action plan in a step-by-step fashion. Sometimes developing a flow-chart helps you better visualize the steps. Using the time line you've established for the goal, set individual completion times for each action step. At this point you may see that the original completion day was a bit too optimistic and some adjustment is needed. That's all right. Actually, you may also see that you've been too generous with your time and you may want to speed things up a bit. Once you've listed all the action steps and the time needed for each step, prioritize them in the proper sequence to maximize your efficiency.

11. *Engage in visualization.* The practice of seeing yourself accomplishing a task before you actually do it is very common on the athletic field. Athletes see themselves completing a task before they actually do it.

30

A reporter covering a track meet noticed a high jumper taking a long time before he moved towards the bar. On one jump, he remained motionless, eyes closed, seemingly distant from the event. After eight minutes, he moved towards the bar and easily cleared the height. That jump won the event.

During an interview following the event, the reporter asked the jumper why he took so long to complete the final jump. His answer was, "I didn't move forward until I saw myself clearing the bar in my mind." He understood the power of visualization.

I am a strong believer in the power of visualization. I use the technique to prepare for every workshop, seminar, or keynote speech I give. I will see myself delivering the program. I picture my gestures, style of delivery, audience reactions—the whole bit. I might add that I expect positive results and I'm never disappointed. Visualization works and helps build expectations.

For each goal you've selected, go through the visualization exercise. Feel the emotions that the process generates. Feel the emotions of accomplishment. The more vivid your visualization, the more you increase your potential to achieve the goal.

12. *Practice daily reinforcement.* Professional speaker Brian Tracy, CSP, CPAE, advocates that you rewrite your goals each morning. I've tried this technique and it does a great job of reinforcing your commitment. It takes just a few minutes and it is a great daily stimulus to action.

13. *Periodically evaluate your position.* At some interval, you must take time to reflect on your progress. I recommend weekly adjustments. You might be more comfortable with a longer period. I would not recommend that you wait more than one month. During these sessions, strive to get an honest appraisal of where you are in the process.

You will make mistakes and you will have to make adjustments. Sometimes you will come across a glaring miscalculation. Don't panic. Make corrections and continue with a positive outlook.

14. *Never give up.* Winston Churchill, while encouraging the British people to hold off Hitler's attacks, told them that victory would be theirs if they simply never gave up. To you I say the same thing—never give up on your dream. If you can sincerely desire something and visualize its reality, it can be yours if you persist long enough. No great act was accomplished with a half-hearted effort. Give it all you have and persist until you are successful.

Napoleon Hill said it best. He said, *"Ask life for great gifts and you encourage life to deliver them to you."* And I seem to remember another source that said, *"Whatsoever you ask in My name, shall be given to you."* Considering *that* source, I believe dreams can come true if you want them badly enough and if you simply ask for them.

How badly do you want to achieve your dreams? Have you asked lately?

Action steps
to
success

1. When have you blamed others for an unsuccessful event?

2. How can you change your perspective about those events and resolve to improve on the future?

3. On page twenty, I listed twelve important questions. Care fully review each one and write your answer.

4. How much time each week do you spend thinking about how to improve all aspects of your life? Schedule time to think about ways to improve.

5. What choices have you made in the last five years that have produced positive results? What choices fell short of your expectations?

6. Complete the personal inventory suggested on page twenty-six.

7. Begin developing a goal list. Use the steps outlined on pages twenty-six through thirty-one.

Notes & thoughts for action.....

Part II

Develop
The
Right Attitude

Key Points:

1. Mistakes are not failures.
2. Encourage rather than criticize.
3. Don't blame others.
4. Get involved.
5. Decide not to be dissatisfied.
6. Be persistent.
7. Attitude affects accomplishments.
8. Win or perish.
9. Desire backed by faith equals commitment.
10. We have met the enemy and it is us.
11. Master your thoughts, master your life.
12. We have the power to choose what happens to us.
13. Life is like a flea market.
14. Throw yourself into your job.
15. We perform according to our perception of our abilities.

If all you do is talk about your bad habits, it's probably because they are the best you have.

How Did The Pot Get Black?

New cookware is bright and shiny; so bright that we can see our reflection on the surface. How do those same pots become stained and black with residue? It's a gradual transition. Little by little, the deposits build until one day we wake up and the pots are black.

Is your life like the black pots? Has the residue of failure and defeat created a black feeling inside? Is the bright and shiny future you once dreamed about now black and dark with gloom? Have the habits that can block future growth slowly crept into your life?

We all experience setbacks. No one is immune to the ravages of defeat. No one can find an excuse for letting those defeats blacken their life. We have the power to overcome any circumstance and bring back that shine.

The process begins by having the desire to stop letting temporary setbacks become permanent. Before any change can occur, you have to want to change and believe that you can. The reality is we become what we think about and desire to be.

What about that bright and shiny future that has turned dull and gray? Things can return to their original state through the use of goals. Giving yourself direction removes the potential for failure. If you can set the goal and cover it with desire, it can be yours. Most settle for much less than they deserve and less than they are capable of achieving. Don't be one who falls into this trap.

40

Actor Christopher Reeves fell from his horse and was left totally paralyzed. That life-changing event could have darkened his outlook and dulled his bright, shiny future. Instead, he turned this black event into dazzling sunshine. His courageous fight to once again gain control of his body is inspiring to all who have followed his story.

Reeves understands that maintaining a bright future is fueled by positive thoughts and actions. He knows that he cannot live with hostility, aggression, fear, or pity dominating his life. If he does, it will become easy to feel sorry for himself.

By moving boldly, Christopher Reeves has kept fear and self-pity out of his life. By sincerely caring for others and placing service to humanity above his troubles, he removed any opportunity for hostility and aggression to cloud his outlook. By setting lofty goals, he has built purpose and direction. He will not let bad habits dull the finish of his cookware!

If your pots have gotten black and you don't know how or why, spend time thinking about these ideas. Restoration is possible and a brightness can once again be yours. It's the winners who bounce back and overcome obstacles. Winners know how to bring purpose to their life. They understand how to make life take on a brightness and shine.

Cynical thoughts on the shortcomings of others are often the very things we wish we had.

If Only

We sometimes fall back on a built-in crutch that we use to make life more bearable. When things don't go right, we reach for this crutch and lament:

"**If only** *I'd been born to wealthier parents, I wouldn't have it so hard.*"

"**If only** *I'd gone to college to further my education, I could advance more rapidly in my job.*"

"**If only** *I lived in another town, the opportunities would be so much better.*"

"**If only** *I'd married that other woman, my marriage would be stronger.*"

"**If only** *I'd gone into another profession, things would be better on the job.*"

"**If only** *my political party were in power, this country would be a better place in which to live.*"

In each of the above examples, we engage in the worst exercise there is—*finger pointing!* We seek to place the blame anywhere but within ourselves.

I hate to be the bearer of bad news, but—it's not anyone's fault for where you are. You've managed to get where you are through your own efforts. Let's revisit each statement listed above to further illustrate the point.

I'm the first to admit that being born to wealth does have its advantages. Yet a lack of wealth and formal education did not stop Henry Ford, Andrew Carnegie, Thomas Edison, Abraham Lincoln, and countless other pioneers who rose to the top in spite of their humble beginnings. None used **if only** as an excuse to fail. They all moved forward and gave life their best effort. They all refused to believe that they could not succeed in their respective fields. A lack of education and money didn't stop their climb to greatness.

Is the grass always greener in the other pasture? Most of the time it is not. If it is, it's probably because the other person is taking better care of his grass. We don't take time to study our own environment to see what it has to offer. Your town can offer lush, green pastures as well. It's not always necessary to go elsewhere to make it. Those who make it in your town understand their own grass holds promise.

What about marriage? Have you done your best at all times to make it work? Examine your role. If you are not getting the treatment you want, examine the treatment you are giving your spouse. You reap what you sow. That's the way it works. So, if things aren't very pleasant and you truly want to salvage your marriage, consider changing your behavior. That move might be what makes the difference. After all, you really don't know if that other woman or man would have changed your situation as long as your behavior is the same.

We often tend to believe that other job opportunities would be so much better. We imagine ourselves in new surroundings but we don't imagine ourselves changing.

The question to ponder is whether or not you have taken advantage of every opportunity your profession offers. Have you taken time to study your craft? How many new things have you learned about your job in the last week? Month? Year? How significant is your job to the survival of your company? How valuable have you made yourself? In most cases, your job offers opportunities to ultimately satisfy your career needs. It may not be the exact job you now hold but, building from that position, you can open doors. It takes preparation and commitment to be a professional at all times.

Today, the favorite game of voters is to blame the party in power for their woes. When the Democrats are in power, we believe Republicans can save the day. When Republicans gain control, give us the Democrats so stability can return. As someone who spent twelve years in an elected public office, I can very candidly tell you that it doesn't matter who is in power. The real issue is how involved voters are with the political process. *Both* parties listen to their constituents. That is the way they make decisions—in the direction of the political winds. And you, my friend, can be a hurricane if you only become involved. The problem is that we don't take time to learn what our elected officials are doing, so they do the most expedient thing they believe will get them reelected. You want to change the political structure? Get involved!

The bottom line? Nobody but you is in charge. If things are not where they ought to be, examine your role. Stop using the **if only** crutch and move on with your life. You can always change. You can always make things better.

Decide that you no longer want to be dissatisfied. There is no barrier you cannot overcome if the determination is great enough. Strong desires have a way of turning dreams into reality. I believe you can have what you want in life if you quit making excuses.

44

The treasures of life are sometimes so obvious that we over-look them.

One Man's Junk Is Another Man's Treasure

There remains within us a bit of the child-like character. We enjoy stumbling onto something seemingly lost, someone's discarded item that we find valuable. I was vividly reminded of this fact during a recent trip through a flea market. As I walked through the thousands of items on display, I couldn't help wondering how many were at one time someone's junk. Old baseball cards, comic books, paperbacks, dishes, glasses, and countless other items were available. We have, at one time or another, thrown similar items out of our house as junk. Now each of these relics, once thought to be worthless, had moved to a new place of prominence and increased in value.

Almost as interesting as the pieces on display were the many people who were rummaging through the piles. Each was looking for that long-awaited bargain, that lost treasure hidden among the many goods before them. Each was looking to turn one man's junk into their pot of gold.

We've often seen this scene repeated in the backyard sales. Seldom does a weekend go by in our community without someone hosting a garage sale. People start at the crack of dawn and park in the streets waiting for the host to open shop. They want to be the first in line. They want to be the first to find that real bargain. The anticipation of the big find motivates. Everybody loves a bargain.

And who can criticize the feeling one gets when such a bargain is acquired? It's always exciting when we acquire something that we've wanted or something that we value highly.

I can remember the years I played in a dance band. It was the time when the old standards such as *Stardust* and *Moonglow* were being replaced by the music of Fats Domino, Bill Haley, and Elvis. *Blue Monday, Rock Around the Clock,* and *All Shook Up* were the tunes we loved. We were the new rock and roll generation and our music was important to us.

Owning those records was every teenager's wish. But for most, money was scarce and buying records was a luxury. At times, the record shops would sell records that had been removed from juke boxes. They were used, but to those of us who had limited funds, finding a popular record at bargain basement prices was exciting. Almost forty years later, these treasures are still in my possession. One man's junk became another man's treasure.

How does all this play into building a successful life? Let's pretend life is like that flea market or that record shop I just described. Like these places, life displays thousands of options from which we can choose. Each has its own price tag. Some are high. Some are cheap. But all have some value. In the flea market, we look carefully and pick the one item we feel will give us the best bargain. In the record shop, I examined the choices and picked my favorites.

In life, we should also look carefully and pick items that help us reach our potential They are our treasures. In the flea market, it takes a sharp eye to pick the best deal. In life, the same screening is needed. Unlike the record shop, life offers us intangibles—things like our feelings, beliefs, attitudes, and persistence to accomplish our goals. Proper use of these bargains of life demand that we have a sharp shopper's eye.

46

We need to know when the most value comes from our feelings and beliefs, and our adherence to them. We need to understand the price we pay for a poor attitude. We need to practice persistence in order to be able to purchase our dreams and reach all our goals.

Winners shop in life's flea market and find the bargain of the day. They pick up the things that losers discard and turn them into their own personal treasure chest.

How do you look upon life? Do you see junk or do you see treasure?

No matter how hard you try, you cannot help people who do not want to help themselves. That is an impossible obstacle.

The Desire To Improve Yourself

Have you ever attended an athletic event that was won by a team far less talented than their opponent? As the contest progresses, it's obvious who will win. When the game is over, the losing team can only lament, "How could this have happened?"

The answer is simple and can be summed up with a one-word response. DESIRE! One team wanted it more than the other. Talent had little to do with the outcome. Desire was the real driver. The less talented winners refused to believe that the odds were against them. And, once again, the underdog won.

In the world of sports, this scene is often repeated. It happens in other arenas as well. In our schools, the student who is not blessed with great brain power somehow plods along and moves on to great academic accomplishments. At work, the seemingly less skilled worker advances through the ranks and serves as a shining example of what desire can do.

Let's look at a contrast. Bob Conklin, founder of the *Adventures in Attitude* self-improvement program, maintains that there will always be slums. There will always be slums because there will always be some number of people who have no desire to leave that type of environment. They do not have the desire to rid themselves of this slum shackle, so they remain hopelessly chained to the walls of dispair.

Living in slums and lacking funds is no disgrace. Sometimes we cannot help the circumstances into which life thrust us. Likewise, not yet having achieved your dream is no disgrace. What should change is acceptance of these circumstances without a desire to improve. What should change is the acceptance of limitations.

In my community, Sister Marie Forgothy labored over fifty years helping the poor. A few years before her death I asked her who would carry on her legacy when she no longer could. Her response was surprising. She told me there would always be poor people. If I wanted to help poor people, I should help educate youngsters. Education was a way to escape being poor.

What Conklin and Sister Marie are saying is that there will always be people who cannot develop the desire to change their circumstance. They are trapped in turmoil and turbulence. They don't understand how to escape. That is a harsh reality of life.

What about you? You may not be living in a slum or be considered poor, but you may want to change your circumstances. How strong is your desire for change? Are you content to remain where you are for the rest of your life?

The story is told of the warrior who sent his armies into battle against almost impossible odds. After he landed his troops on the enemy's shore, he burned his ships. Speaking to his shocked soldiers, he told them that they could not leave these shores alive unless they won. They had no choice—it was either win or perish! *They won!*

Can you adopt the attitude of those soldiers? It is desire, backed by strong action, that makes things happen and leads to success.

Sometimes a look in the mirror is all it takes to see the enemy.

Your Self-concept And Success

We are always responsible for everything we think, say, do, or feel. We alone have the power to choose what happens to us. Often, we shortchange ourselves because we believe we are less than we actually are. *We are the enemy!*

It's important to have faith in our abilities, to believe in ourselves. Now, I'm not suggesting conceit—that rare disease affecting everyone but the person who has it. Rather, I want to build a reasonable confidence in your own power to reach your goals. How can you do this? Success begins when we learn what it takes to build a stronger self-concept.

We don't perform according to our actual abilities. We perform according to our perception of our abilities. Noted psychologist, Dr. Joyce Brothers, in a *Parade* magazine article says, *"An individual's self-concept is the core of their personality. It affects every aspect of human behavior—the ability to learn, the capacity to grow and change, the choice of mates, friends, and career. It's no exaggeration to say that a strong, positive self-image is the best possible preparation for success in life."*

Dr. Brothers is referring to the blueprint we have of our abilities. We have our own perceived set of plans, our own life-building code. Rarely do we question its validity. We follow the plan and allow that blueprint to control every talent we have.

50

If possessing the right blueprint is so important, what can we do to improve ourselves? Experts have many opinions but there is a central theme in every theory—*we must learn to control the way we think!* Earl Nightingale, in his classic audio "The Strangest Secret," concluded that we become what we think about.

Our thoughts program our subconscious mind, the storehouse of all impressions. The subconscious accepts, without question, all thoughts received and stores them for future use. By repeating thoughts often enough, we assemble the blueprint for our belief system. Soon, right or wrong, our thoughts build our reality and become a major influence on the construction of our self-concept.

By properly controlling our thinking, we can eventually correct falsely developed deficiencies and turn our negative thinking around. By mastering our thoughts, we begin to master our life. The end result of this process is a blueprint that we can use to build a strong house. All the huffing and puffing by the big bad wolf—your wrong beliefs—will never blow your house down.

Don't add difficulties to your life by fabricating a poor self-concept of your abilities. Be a master architect working from correctly drawn plans. That is the only way to complete your house of success.

The game of life can bring great pleasures when we under-stand the rules by which we should play.

Some Guiding Principles

Here is a list of principles that, if put in place, will do much to help you in your search for success. Each is deceptively simple yet amazingly powerful and needs no further explanation.

Don't speed through the list. Give each item the thought it deserves. As you think about a principle, exam the value it has in your life or how you might more fully incorporate it into your daily activities. Writing your thoughts will give you a permanent record that can be modified and ultimately crafted into your philosophy of living. Now that is a powerful thought!

1. Always practice integrity in everything you do.
2. Think and plan using a pen and paper.
3. Develop written goals.
4. Love God, yourself, your family, and your fellow man.
5. Make the world a better place.
6. Always do your best, no matter the activity. Stay prepared.
7. Life's greatest treasures cannot be bought.
8. Take time to smell the roses.
9. Reflect on and evaluate your activities each day.
10. Don't judge. Don't discriminate.
11. Forgive and forget.
12. Always do the important things.
13. Don't take yourself too seriously. Occasionally act silly.
14. Give, expecting nothing in return.

52

15. Finish what you start.
16. Do it now.
17. Listen.
18. Be responsible, creative and patient.
19. Dare to be different.
20. Teach when you can.
21. Value people, not things.
22. Exercise and eat right.
23. Write.
24. Talk to your family.
25. Treat animals with kindness.
26. Sing in the shower.
27. Be happy. Smile a lot.
28. Cry when you are sad.
29. Save a portion of everything you earn.
30. Keep a neat desk.
31. Rest when you are sick.
32. Pray each day.
33. Keep telling everyone you love that you do.
34. Take pride in yourself.
35. Dream big. Take risks.
36. Learn something new every day.
37. Get a hobby.
38. Go to church every Sunday.
39. Read part of a book every day.
40 Think safety in everything you do.
41. Enjoy your work.
42. Find your purpose.

Add any principles you feel are important. From time to time, you may want to review the thoughts you've recorded to help keep your focus in the right direction. Happy searching!

Action steps
to
success

1. Do you engage in self pity? If so, what can you do to stop this self-destructive habit?

2. What "If only" excuse have you been making? What are you going to do to change?

3. How would others classify your attitude—positive or negative? Ask a few honest friends for their opinion.

4. What is the one area of your life that could stand the most improvement? How will you approach this change?

5. How do you feel about your ability to reach success? Do you believe you can achieve your strongest desire?

6. Examine your thinking pattern. Do you engage in negative self-talk? How might you change those conversations to a more positive communication with yourself?

7. Thoroughly examine each principle discussed on pages fifty-one and fifty-two.

Notes & thoughts
for action.....

Part III

Develop A Career, Not A Job

Key Points:

1. Do more than is expected of you.
2. Have guidelines for handling change.
3. Be a professional on the job.
4. Life is too short to work at a miserable job.
5. Find satisfaction with your work.
6. Look for opportunities.
7. Find opportunities to do what is not being done.
8. Consistent management style is best.
9. Develop a winning résumé.
10. Make job interviews positive.

Doing an ordinary activity in an extra-ordinary fashion is the way to build excellence.

Going The Extra Mile

Are you satisfied with your current income? My guess is if you are reading these words, you are not! And that's good. Satisfaction has never created great things. It's only the restless nature of human beings that brings forth creation.

Here is a formula that will help you move up the financial ladder. I call it, *"Going the extra mile."* Let me illustrate with this question. If you just do what you are paid to do, should you get a raise? There are those who will say that longevity deserves compensation. I believe differently. If you've done nothing to increase your value to your employer, why should you get more money? Eventually, your employer will be no better off and will have no extra funds. You will both be out of a job.

If you own your own business, the same philosophy applies. Giving your customers more than they expect will generate more business and help keep the customer base you grow. I'm sure you know businesses that go the extra mile to serve and satisfy their customers. I certainly remember a man who practiced that philosophy.

Mr. Joe Casso owned his own service station. It wasn't a big, fancy place. There was a small, congested, room in the front of the building where business was conducted. The rear portion was his home. Only two pumps were available to pump gas. To the side of his place stood a rack for changing oil, mufflers, and doing minor repairs.

As you drove up to his station, chances are you would see Mr. Joe disassembling large truck or tractor tires with *hand* tools, changing oil, or making some minor repair. He would stop his task, rush to the gasoline pump, and begin filling your tank. While the tank was filling, he would open the hood and check the water, battery, wires, and whatever else he could inspect. If your hood or door squeaked when it opened, out came the can of oil or a small amount of grease. The windows were cleaned and the air pressure checked in each tire.

Everyone received the same treatment no matter how much the purchase. Mr. Joe knew how to go the extra mile and keep his customers coming back. The value of his efforts rewarded him with a steady business and loyal customers. I did business with Mr. Joe for about fifteen years. When he closed his place, the world lost a shining example of superior customer care.

Compensation in the work place should be based purely on value. It doesn't matter if you work for someone else or if you are self-employed like Mr. Joe. Increased value equals increased compensation. That's what you get from going the extra mile!

I don't want to just equate the extra mile concept with money. The principle holds true for every other facet of life. It is impossible to render service and not be compensated. What you receive may take on many forms and come from many sources but the return will be yours. The principle never fails to deliver.

Do you shop with the merchant who provides that little extra or do you frequent establishments that are indifferent to your business? What about friends? Aren't they the people you can depend on when you need someone? Look in your work environment. Promotable people are those who separate themselves from the average worker because they do the little extras.

Consider how you might use this principle to help move your career up a bit or to help build your business if you are self-employed. Emulate Mr. Joe's approach to his customers. Do the little bit extra that is not expected.

Following the principle of the extra mile will reward you far beyond monetary compensation. The rewards for such a lifestyle are priceless. Happiness and prosperity are yours when you make doing the little extras part of your daily activities. The search for success is much shorter with such an attitude.

Most people resist change. But without change, we would still be living in caves.

Implementing Change In A Positive Way

Today, the business climate is undergoing turbulent times. Downsizing, reengineering, reduction in force, reorganization—it doesn't matter what term you use. They all mean the same thing—change is occurring. To survive, we need to learn how to deal effectively with change. Here are a few thoughts to help you and your organization make transitions smoother.

As a worker, keep abreast of what is happening in the company. Learn how the business is run. Learn all you can about the industry in which you work. This information will better prepare you for any upcoming change. Many times, you become aware of the potential for change before it occurs, giving you time to prepare for future adjustments.

Organizations should not change just for change's sake. There should always be a legitimate reason for implementing any change. The primary reason many organizations introduce change is to increase the bottom line. Even promotions are designed to increase efficiency. The intended result of promoting a worker is better operation of a department and eventual cost savings. Reductions in the number of workers is also intended to increase profits. While this activity is not a pleasant experience, let's face it, if a company does not make a profit, there is no reason for it to exist. Sometimes that requires hard choices.

When any change is implemented, people usually react from an emotional level rather than a logical position. If you are in charge of implementing change, prepare people for the change. Don't just spring the change and expect universal acceptance. Involve people who are going to be affected by change. Ask for their help, and if they offer a better idea, use it. Ownership reduces resistance and makes change more palatable.

Some years ago, I was managing a laboratory. We were given funds to renovate the lab. At first, I was going to design the changes *I wanted to implement* independent of the technicians who actually worked in the lab on a day-to-day basis. After all, I was the boss and knew what was best for my workers!

Through sheer luck or a stroke of managerial genius, I changed my mind and decided to let the technicians offer design options. When the project was complete, I had only picked the color and style of cabinets. The entire layout was done by the technicians. Because they were involved, the final design was far superior to any design I could have done by myself. More importantly, no one has complained about the design since it was completed. Ownership does reduce resistance and makes change more palatable.

Workers have a responsibility to cooperate with the company in a positive fashion while change is being implemented. Don't be hasty to react negatively. The natural tendency is to resist, but a cooperative spirit does more good than harm. This may be particularly hard when change involves reclassification of job responsibilities. Such change may be beyond worker control. That is reality. Employees should do the best they can to work through it. There may be difficulties, but a commitment to work with your company produces less tension and makes any transition smoother.

There are times when an organization must implement change prior to notifying employees. Under these circumstances, managers should be prepared to discuss the change with their people as early as possible. Maintaining a positive approach helps workers accept the change in a more positive way. Companies should stress the benefits to workers. Workers should look for the new opportunities created by change.

Sometimes change is made more difficult by the rumor mill. The underground network can cause much grief for a company or manager trying to change some part of their operation. If untruths surface, put a stop to them. That may mean sharing some information about the upcoming change before you may have intended to do so. Better to be a bit premature than face a hostile work force when you finally implement the change. Workers on the other hand should understand that rumors are often just that—rumors. Consider the source before you react to rumors. Exercise caution before you let your emotions rise.

Any time a change is implemented, proponents should do a thorough job of explaining who is affected, why the change was introduced, and how the change will be implemented. This provides another opportunity to emphasize the positive side of the change.

Several years ago, the Governor of Louisiana proposed a state-wide teacher evaluation program. This new initiative was going to rid our state of bad teachers and hold the rest accountable. As the Governor presented the program, almost every statement contained a negative commentary. Soon teachers across the state were frightened and resistance surfaced at every turn. Almost all the rules for implementing change were violated. There was no successful dialog between government, teachers, school boards, legislators, parents, universities, business leaders, and teacher unions.

From the beginning, the teacher evaluation program was doomed to fail. Even the strong points of the program could not hold back the wave of controversy and emotional upheaval that built up. The result was total failure and a huge waste of tax-payer funds.

Sometimes, acceptance of change takes time. Be prepared for the delay. Don't expect workers to be overjoyed with every change. No matter how positive, some workers will challenge the need for change. Be sensitive to such issues and be prepared to deal with them. Speak to those who don't accept the change. You may find a good reason to modify the change during such conversations. If that occurs, be prepared to make concessions. Had this process been followed with the ill-fated teacher evaluation program, it might have survived.

Like most events in life, timing is important. When you implement change can be as important as the change itself. Consider all factors involved when contemplating change. Look for the best conditions and time before you move.

Once change is introduced, proper follow-up is critical. Many times, changes are made and workers are left fending for themselves. With no opportunity for feedback, resistance builds, and the reaction can become explosive. We have seen too many cases in recent times where worker retaliation has produced fatal consequences. Keep an eye on what reaction is occurring in the work force and do all you can to prevent future difficulties.

Some years ago, I was involved in the implementation of a no smoking policy. Our committee elected to totally ban smoking. We were also going to offer assistance to smokers to help them break the habit. As non-smokers, we thought it was a workable plan. But to the smokers, there were no options. We had not given the smokers an opportunity to express their feelings and soon resistance surfaced.

66

We set up a series of meetings to hear their side. Once the dialog started, options developed. Smokers were given a special place to smoke outside of the buildings and non-smokers did not have to be exposed to second hand smoke. By engaging in dialog, each side won something in the negotiations and a very emotional change was successfully implemented.

A final thought. If you made a wrong change, be big enough to admit it and take the necessary corrective action. Nothing could be worse than ignoring a bad change. Admitting you made a mistake only makes you human. That admission could be the best morale builder you could implement.

As Charles Kettering said, *"The world hates change, yet it is the only thing that has brought progress."* If an organization is to grow, it has a responsibility to change. Accepting that fact makes for less heartache when change comes. Anytime you are involved in a change, either as the recipient or promoter, be willing to accept the progress that can be gained. If done properly, with thorough study and considerations, change can be a very positive force along the path of success.

Never approach your work with a half-hearted effort. Give it all you have and you will be rewarded with great satisfaction and growth.

Some Thoughts About Work

I've got a question for you. What would make you quit your job more readily: (1) working a job that was too easy, or (2) working a job that was too challenging?

If you chose number one, you are in agreement with a majority of workers. They repeatedly say that a challenging job is what they want and that they were more likely to leave a less challenging situation than one that was demanding.

At first thought, one might be inclined to think that working at a job with little or no responsibility is the ideal job choice. This might be acceptable for awhile. However, boredom and dissatisfaction would eventually surface. This situation would prompt most workers to make the choice to seek other employment.

There is satisfaction when one is doing a challenging task. The feeling of pride and accomplishment from having done a good job is exhilarating. This thought was amplified by a group of workers I surveyed during a quality training program. From among a list of choices, they selected doing challenging work as one of their top two choices—far ahead of good pay! The other choice was developing a feeling of pride about their work. Think about your work situation. Is it challenging your abilities or can you coast through it each day with great ease? Do you feel a sense of pride at the end of the day because you engaged in meaningful work?

68

No matter what you do for a living, you owe it to yourself to find satisfaction in your work. Life is too short to work at a miserable job. If unhappiness occurs on the job, that feeling will carry itself off the job and ultimately affect your family relations. That is too steep a price to pay for job misery. Don't misunderstand this message. I am not advocating that you immediately terminate your employment if you are dissatisfied with your current position. What I am suggesting is that you need to find satisfaction in your work. If you can't quit and you're unhappy, what can you do? Here are some suggestions that can help. See how many you can adapt to your work situation to make it more meaningful and satisfying.

1. *Every day, try to do things a little better than the day before.* Sometimes, with a little more effort, we can raise our level of competency and vastly improve the quality of our work. It's the little things that make the big difference. This practice may separate you from the masses and ultimately lead to a promotion.

2. *Go beyond the routine.* "I only do what they tell me to do." That's the dialogue of a loser. Examine your job and see how you might make it more creative, exciting, rewarding, and fun. It is possible to create enthusiasm for any job.

3. *Be a pro.* Professionals always perform at the peak of their abilities. To be a pro, you must first think like a pro. Professional athletes are expected to give it their all every moment they are in a contest. Those who choose to do it differently find themselves out of work. There is something very satisfying about doing things well. The professionals understand this and perform well on every occasion.

This year professional basketball fans witnessed an outstanding performance by Michael Jordan of the Chicago Bulls. Michael left basketball for two years and attempted to make a transition into professional baseball. He was not successful.

When it became evident that he would not make the transition into baseball, Jordan came back to his game, basketball. With the heart of a champion, he worked and worked to regain his basketball skills. After two years, he led his team to the best NBA record of all times and another championship. Jordan was again voted the league's outstanding player. He is a pro in every sense of the word.

4. *Get ready for opportunity.* Think of opportunity as a freeway. All the blue colored cars traveling this freeway carry an opportunity to improve your life. The others do nothing for you. You have the ability to stop any car you wish but you haven't trained yourself to recognize the color blue. Without that knowledge, finding opportunity is very difficult. You can randomly stop a car and hope it contains the riches you seek but the odds are working against you. However, when you prepare yourself to "see the blue," you are better able to stop the right car and capture its riches. Prepare yourself because you never know when a blue car might pass by.

5. *Acquire reference materials about your work.* Be constantly looking for any source of information that will enlighten you about your work. The source might come from a formal course or could simply be an article in a magazine. Learn all you can about your job and the industry in which you work. You never know when the information might prove beneficial. Staying abreast of new discoveries, trends and the thinking of leaders in your field, is also an excellent practice to implement.

6. *The grass isn't always greener on the other side of the fence.* At times, we have the perception that moving to another position will bring us the happiness and satisfaction we seek from our work. While that can be the case, look carefully before you leap. What looks good on the surface, with further examination, might actually prove to be a worse situation.

70

Take time to explore all possibilities that exist in your current employment before you cast your eyes on new territory. If none exist, then you can begin to exercise other options.

Fredrick Buechner, in his book, *Wishful Thinking,* describes finding our ideal vocation this way: *"The place God calls you is the place where your deep gladness and the world's deep hunger meet."* I cannot offer you better advice to help with your search for success in your career choice.

The key to building an excellent management style is to always be willing to do the things you ask others to do for you.

You're A Boss In Trouble If You...

Whether you are working full time in a management position. or you don't supervise anyone, use these twenty tips as a valuable addition to your professional development plan.

You are a boss in trouble if you—

1. Take sole credit for the accomplishments of the people you supervise or if you never pass on their contributions to upper management.

2. Fail or refuse to give employees the opportunity to grow professionally or discuss their goals and performance.

3. Reprimand a worker in front of his or her peers.

4. Take personally an honest disagreement from one of your workers or if you never admit that you could be wrong on an issue.

5. Try to cover up mistakes made by workers, in order to gain favor with your superiors.

6. Do not have a sense of humor or can laugh at yourself.

7. Protect your favorite worker's poor performance by overlooking glaring errors that will come back to haunt him and you!

8. Die on the job or simply give up improving. Some people call this dying before you're dead.

9. Criticize poor performance without offering insight for improvement or feedback on why the performance is unacceptable.

10. Rob people of their ability to enjoy their jobs because you never delegate, let them solve their own problems, or, in some cases, actually do the employee's work.

11. Make promises that you can't make good in order to invigorate job performance.

12. Let political decisions influence promotions rather than good performance; promote the good old boy over the most competent performer.

13. Avoid ever hearing the truth about what is going on within the organization because you've surrounded yourself with "yes" men.

14. Only comment on mistakes and never praise good performance.

15. Hold back the potential of a superior performer simply because they are too young.

16. Don't let your superiors know about outstanding performance within your department.

17. Don't share your knowledge with workers, or horde information because you want to be the only one able to perform an activity.

18. Insufficiently train people prior to and after moving them in a position of managerial responsibility.

19. Maintain a closed-door policy and never provide employees the opportunity to speak to you when the need arises.

20. Never take time to reflect on your performance or the performance of people you manage.

Use these suggestions to shorten your learning curve to successfully manage people.

A worker who only does what he or she is paid to do will never get paid more then they deserve.

The Secret To Getting Promoted

Everyone strives for a successful career. We all want advancements and opportunities to use our talents and skills. If you work at a job that doesn't maximize your abilities, you don't have to continue working under these conditions. There is a process you can use that can lead to advancements, more income, and increased responsibility. I've tested its validity for the past twenty-seven years. Without any hesitation, I can tell you it works.

What is this magic formula? Well, there's no trickery or deception involved. It's actually fairly straightforward and will work in virtually any profession. All you do is follow this rule:

Look around your place of employment for a responsibility that you could do that is not now being done by anyone. Then, ask permission to do it.

The younger the organization in which you work, the more choices should be available. Sometimes, in a mature organization, some very basic things are not functioning as well as they could or some very obvious gaps exist in the structure of a department. The key here is to build an awareness of what is going on and to have the vision to see what can be improved.

A second consideration is to accurately assess your strengths to see exactly how you can contribute. Sometimes it will mean additional schooling. Be ready to do what you must to acquire skills for advancement when opportunities present themselves.

Lastly, if you've established a reputation for doing your job professionally, asking for more responsibility will generally be greeted with little resistance. Top management likes to see initiative and concern for the welfare of the company. Don't be afraid to ask if you've laid the proper groundwork.

Allow me to outline for you the steps and activities I initiated in the twenty-seven years spent in an industrial setting.

When I began my career as a chemist in 1969, it was in a new chemical company. On this job, routine analyses were performed on process vessels and finished product. Two things I did were ask permission to order supplies and ask permission to organize the equipment so routine testing could be done more efficiently. These were not major undertakings but no one had been assigned this responsibility.

Within two years, I was moved from shift work to a day position as a project chemist. At the same time, we hired four technicians to monitor the loading activities for a new production facility. Since part of my work entailed analyses of shipments to customers, I asked permission to set up this lab and to establish the analytical schedule. For the next two years, I supervised these activities even though I was not in a management position. I also organized a test-method manual because no formal document existed.

Four and one-half years after beginning my employment, I was asked to move to another company within the complex as the lab supervisor. One month after moving into this new position, the first EPA water permit was issued. That opened the door for environmental responsibilities.

Sensing that environmental concerns were here to stay, I asked permission to become involved and easily gained this responsibility. My studies of environmental issues continued until I was able to take sole management responsibilities for all corporate environmental requirements.

When I moved to the new position, we had no one at the site providing technical service to our customers. We relied upon the services of a chemist in one of our parent companies. This individual was extremely competent but did not work in our complex. Another need surfaced.

The chemistry used in our industry was very complex and there was limited written reference material available to study. It took me several years to gain the confidence to move forward with this second need. By 1979, I felt ready enough to develop a technical service program, so I asked permission to do so. To my dismay, the idea was rejected. Some months later a breakthrough opportunity developed.

I received a desperate call for help from a customer on a Friday afternoon. They wanted someone to visit their facility on Monday to provide technical assistance. I called the president of our company and asked permission to visit the customer. I was given the green light.

After a review of the situation on Monday morning, the cause of their difficulties was identified. Unfortunately, the solution required a smaller particle size product that we currently produced. With a team effort at our facility, we were able to produce a small quantity of product meeting their particle size requirements.

The end result? Creation of a new product line, a satisfied customer who was able to meet a contract requirement, the successful establishment of a technical service program, a letter of appreciation from our customer for the effort we put forth, and a promotion for me.

As the quality issue began to become more and more prominent, another need arose. We needed a plant-wide quality system. By asking, I was given permission to begin the development of a corporate mission statement and a formal quality process. Both were in place by 1985.

Within a few years, ISO 9000 quality requirements began to gain momentum. Sensing that this issue was going to eventually impact our sales position, I asked for permission to initiate registration under the ISO guidelines. By late 1993, we were ready for the certification audit and on January 4, 1994, we were officially an ISO 9000 registered corporation.

During the same early 1990's period, I was asked to manage the entire safety program for a short period. Within two years and with the help of a great staff, we were able to make significant improvements to our safety program. The current management staff has continued the momentum and each year our safety program gets stronger and stronger.

None of the above is written to impress you about my accomplishments. Many could have done a better job. My primary reason for going into so much detail is to emphasize how developing a vision for what needs to be done can produce dramatic improvements.

Look around your place of employment for a responsibility that you could do that is not now being done by anyone. Then, ask permission to do it.

It's a simple but important rule to remember as you seek to build a successful career.

Work is most satisfying when job activities match our talents and skills.

How To Find And Keep A Job

Part of building a successful life is maintaining gainful employment. Those who learn to position themselves well have an advantage over the casual job seeker. There is an art to applying for a job. Learn it well and your success ratio takes a dramatic shift.

In today's volatile business climate, knowing how to successfully hunt for a job can be a real asset. Here are some thoughts on the two major parts of the process, the application and the interview.

The Application

Some companies require applicants to complete the application form on the company site. If you find yourself in this situation, be sure you practice your best penmanship. Reviewers want to see a neat, legible form. Misspelled words and incorrect grammar can be red flags. I always advocate that if you are not sure of a spelling, either use a dictionary to verify spelling or use a synonym.

All individuals you list as references should be aware that you listed them. Speak to these individuals prior to going for the interview. Tell them about the job you are seeking. This gives them the opportunity to prepare should someone call. Never let a referred person get a cold call from a prospective employer. That always diminishes the impact.

In some situations, you have the added benefit of sub-mitting a résumé. If you submit a résumé, use it as a position-ing tool. Here are some guidelines that will help you present your best self.

1. Include an attention-grabbing cover letter. It should be one page and crisp in content. Include items such as why you are writing, the position you are seeking, and why you want this particular job. You should state what you bring to the com-pany and the response you expect. That's a lot to pack on one page. When you do this effectively, it is a powerful punch and a door opener.

2. Misspelled words, smudges, pages out of sequence, typographical errors, and incorrect grammar are all unforgivable errors.

3. Be sure to include any information that demonstrates leadership or management responsibilities. If you are a recent high school graduate, include extracurricular activities in which you held leadership positions.

4. Don't try to impress anyone with your creativity or writing style. Straightforward, business commentary is best.

5. Include specific work experiences, community serv-ice, and educational accomplishments that would be beneficial to the job requirements.

6. Encourage the reviewer to interview you. That is done in two ways, by the quality of your application and by asking for the interview.

The Interview

If you make the cut and are called in for an interview, the following practices will be beneficial.

1. Be on time. Never make the interviewer wait for you. Better to be thirty minutes early than one minute late.

2. Dress nicely. Men should wear a suit and ladies should wear a nice dress or suit. This is not jeans and T-shirt time.

3. Display your best manners. Politeness is always appreciated and is an attention grabber.

4. When engaged in dialog, vary your word choice and present your ideas in an organized fashion. Take a few seconds to respond rather than blurting out the answer at the speed of light. Sometimes a few seconds to compose your thoughts can increase the quality of your answer. If you are familiar with the industry, use their terms when appropriate. Remember that a good interviewer will let you speak 90% of the time. So be at your best.

5. Listen, listen, listen. The worst thing you can do is give the wrong response because you simply were not listening well.

6. When answering, be accurate, truthful, and as intelligent as possible. If unclear about a question, ask for a clarification. However, it's not a good idea to do this too much during the interview.

7. Ask all the questions you need to be sure you know what you are getting into. If possible, do some research on the company, its products or services, and possible future direction. Annual reports are good sources of such information.

8. As much as possible, apply for work that relates to your qualifications. The better the match, the better the possibilities of employment.

9. Relax. Take a few deep breaths before you start the interview. Don't smoke or fidget in your chair. Act friendly.

10. Strive to build a career rather than just look for a job. There is a big difference and interviewers can sense your position by the information you share. Most companies are looking for a long-term commitment.

80

11. Be prepared, positive, persistent, and professional.

12. If you want the job, ask for it.

13. Thank the interviewer for his or her time when the session is over.

14. Regardless of the outcome, send a thank you note. It's not a bad idea to write it upon exiting the interview and dropping it at the post office on your return trip home. It's impressive to receive a thank you note in the next day's mail.

Few people are born with sufficient resources to never hold a job. During the course of one's lifetime, most will have to go through a job interview. If you happen to currently be in that posture, reread this chapter and position yourself for greater success by adopting the ideas shared. It's an essential step in your search for success.

Action steps

to

success

1. List ways in which you might incorporate "Going the extra mile" concepts in your work environment.

2. Are there significant changes occurring in your work place? If so, what can you do to cope with them in a positive fashion? What can you do to help others cope?

3. Are you satisfied with the profession you've chosen? If not, what can you do to increase your satisfaction level? Look around your place of employment for a responsibility you can do that is not now being done by anyone. Ask permission to do it.

4. What new information have you learned about your work in the last year? Do you keep up with industry trends?

5. Reread to the quote on page seventy. What deep gladness do you possess that would satisfy a deep hunger of the world?

6. Use the suggestions on pages seventy-one and seventy-two to develop a self- improvement plan.

Notes & thoughts
for action.....

Part IV

Two Important Keys To Success—Discipline And Persistence

Key Points:

1. Respect the dignity of all.
2. Keep your word.
3. Practice sincerity.
4. Compete against yourself.
5. False beliefs build barriers.
6. Acknowledge your talents.
7. Decide to take charge of your life.
8. Reject destructive habits.
9. Respect others.
10. Keep good company.

Those with great character are unwilling to abuse power.

Power

Power has many definitions. It can pertain to a force used to do work. It can be the product obtained by multiplying one number by itself a particular number of times. Power can be the amount that an optical lens magnifies. These applications all fit into the category of some scientific definition of power.

There is another form of power I'd like to consider. In this form, power refers to control, authority, and influence. Most think about this form when the word power is mentioned. I'm certain when you read the title of this article the same thought went through your mind.

If you study the life cycle of people, you will see many displays of power. The young child attempting to get his or her way with their parents or sibling is engaged in a power play. The desire for control, authority, and influence begins early.

As we get older, we practice this need for power with our friends. Getting our way is an age-old attempt to gain power. We seek to influence and control who will be our friend and how they will interact with us. It's a game we have all played.

Power is an integral part of the business setting. There is a manager or supervisor who has power over your career and daily work activities. Working for someone who abuses their power can be a living nightmare. These people give no thought to the trail of bodies they walk over and abuse.

88

Perhaps the most blatant use of power is in the political world. It is found in your community and extends to Washington and the world. Every day we see evidence of misuse of power in these arenas. True, the media has increased its monitoring efforts, but in spite of this heightened awareness of political activities, the game continues. The ultimate example of political power is war, the most destructive human activity ever conceived by humans.

On the other hand, power can be a very positive force. This is where people should concentrate their efforts. In all arenas of the world, positive use of power could be the most beneficial practice ever undertaken by humans. Here are a few examples of how it might work:

1. *Go out of your way to help others.* Another way to spell love is h-e-l-p. Many of you know people within your community who exemplify this use of power. They are always there to support and help. They always seem to have time for others. They display positive power.

2. *Never use your position for personal gain at another's expense.* We get privileges by virtue of our position. It's extremely important not to abuse these privileges. We should look for ways to increase our service. By doing so, we get all the personal satisfaction we could ever want. Seems like I remember someone saying that, *"It is in giving that we receive."*

3. *Have respect for the dignity of every other person on earth.* Put another way, if you can't say anything or think anything decent about someone, don't speak or think. Never slight someone because they lack the economic privileges many are blessed with or because their nationality, skin color, or gender is different. Dignity and diversity should be treated as synonyms. Proper practice of this type of power would change the entire complexion of human relations for the better.

4. *Never play favorites.* The rule that will do most to keep you out of trouble is to be consistent in your dealings with people. It doesn't matter if it's friend or foe. Fair and equitable treatment is never the wrong move.

My high school principal, Mr. Clifford Barbier, was a shining example of this practice. Every student knew exactly what would happen when they broke a rule. Every student who broke a rule received the same justice. It didn't matter who your parents were. You could count on his consistency.

5. *Always keep your word.* Become someone who can be depended upon. Promise only what you can deliver, but when you promise, be ready to do whatever it takes to meet your obligation.

6. *Be sincere.* This is one of the most important positive displays of power. Being genuine is a spiritual power that is appreciated by everyone.

Socrates once said, *"Unwillingness to surrender power is the curse of civilization, the root of ages of trouble. Some men find the appetite irresistible. They will sacrifice everything else to hold their power."*

Maintaining the proper balance regarding power will help you reap the rewards the world offers to all who understand its proper application. It's a giant step towards controlling your life. It's a giant step in your search for success.

To live a worthy life, one must be willing to labor and work through pain. Mixing these with persistence and courage will ultimately lead to better things.

Self~Competition

We live in a competitive society. Every facet of our life is, in some way, tied to competition. The moment of conception is the result of a fierce struggle between sperm cells. Competition begins early!

After birth, competition can take the form of sibling rivalries, academic achievements, sporting activities, boy-girl relationships, and job-seeking opportunities. We even carry our obsession to a spectator role. We watch people in competition. It's probably safe to say that our entire life is spent in the presence of some form of competition.

There's another form of competition that I'd like to address. It's a form that most people never recognize. They believe competition means going through life competing against the other fellow. In reality, the only competition they should practice is against themselves.

Self-competition is an activity that produces true improvement. Beating the competition is not as important as beating your own previous personal best at doing an activity. By continually striving to improve the task, we will automatically get better. This is competition at its best. Take a few minutes to reflect on that thought. Think about a situation when you did your best. Wasn't the driving force wanting to improve on your last performance? Let me illustrate the point by carrying the concept one step further.

One of the most productive and skilled leaders history has ever produced was once in trouble. As a young man, he had great difficulty relating to people. Fortunately, he was perceptive enough to know that he needed to change. How did he change? He identified thirteen qualities that he had to acquire in order to improve. He began a little self-competition.

His formula was relatively simple. He practiced one new habit each week. With thirteen characteristics, he was able to practice one per week and repeat the exercise four times a year. In time, by evaluating his effectiveness and improving his processes, he was able to transform himself into a world leader. His self-competition made the difference. Perhaps you've heard of him. His name—*Benjamin Franklin!*

When Franklin embarked on his new journey, he was on the brink of failure. Once he mastered the thirteen qualities, he moved to successes few have duplicated. Had he not changed and begun this form of self-competition, history would have totally ignored him. What a shame that would have been.

What new skills must you acquire to continue your path toward personal growth? Why not write your own improvement list and practice like Franklin. Continue the cycle until the new skills become part of your personality.

It takes no more effort to aim high, to demand abundance and prosperity, than to acquire misery and poverty. It takes no more work on your part to master successful techniques than it will to acquire habits that can only lead to failure.

On the next page, I've provided a list of the thirteen habits Franklin used to improve his success ratio. After you've read through the list, adopt those you like, add your favorite, and begin using your list of thirteen habits.

Happy changing!

Ben Franklin's Thirteen Week Plan

1. **TEMPERANCE:** Franklin set the goal to drink and eat in moderation.
2. **SILENCE:** He recognized the greatness of being silent. His vow was to avoid gossip and trifling conversation.
3. **ORDER:** The focus was on organization of his daily schedule of activities and on having a place for everything.
4. **RESOLUTION:** Franklin put into practice the avoidance of procrastination—the thief of time!
5. **FRUGALITY:** A penny saved is a penny earned. He recognized that control of his finances was critical.
6. **INDUSTRY:** Becoming effective with his time was the major goal. Don't do unnecessary activities. Concentrate on the most important task of the day. Don't waste time.
7. **SINCERITY:** Be honest and just. Speak from the heart.
8. **JUSTICE:** Do no harm to others. Treat people fairly.
9. **MODERATION:** Franklin avoided extremes.
10. **CLEANLINESS:** Keep your body, clothes and habits clean.
11. **TRANQUILLITY:** Avoid acting in a stressful manner. Don't let the trifles of life get to you.
12. **CHASTITY:** I believe no further explanation is needed here.
13. **HUMILITY:** He advocated imitating the life of Jesus and Socrates, probably the two greatest teachers of all time.

Doubting yourself will tarnish your silver lining.

The Invisible Barriers

I don't know how many of you remember the track star, Roger Bannister. To refresh your memory, Roger was the first person to run the mile in less than four minutes. When Bannister first talked about breaking the four-minute barrier, every authority on running came forth with a list of reasons why it could not be done. They went to great lengths to explain why the human body could not stand such a strain. They believed the heart would simply quit pumping. To maintain a pace of less than sixty seconds per quarter mile was unthinkable. I can recall reading many such articles myself and believing that *it was so!*

One person refused to believe those ideas. Roger Bannister believed he could break the barrier. It didn't matter that no one had ever run a mile in less than four minutes. He believed he could and methodically planned every step of the race, never losing sight of his goal. In the end, he reached it.

After Bannister broke the barrier, others began to do it. Once he proved it was possible, the invisible barrier was gone forever. The impossible became easy to do.

How many self-limiting barriers have you placed in your path to a successful life? How often have you doubted your abilities? What activity have you failed to begin because you didn't believe you could complete it? How would your life be different if you could remove those invisible barriers? These are important questions to consider as you seek to improve your life.

Breaking barriers requires belief. Often beliefs get clouded with untruths and we are unable to see ourselves victorious. To clear up the fog of misconceptions, we must be willing to risk failure. We must be willing to question our beliefs so we can venture forward. We must be willing to systematically plan, examine, and evaluate our performance in order to improve the next try. Roger Bannister cleared his foggy misconceptions, he took the risk to fail, he planned every minute detail and, in the end, he proved the world wrong.

Now is the time to start your own demolition company. Now is the time to tear down those walls of limitations and reach for your dream race like Bannister did. You have an abundance of talents. Your resources are barely tapped, no matter how much you've managed to accomplish so far. Resolve to increase your efforts and dig up those untapped resources.

Do not become one of the many that go to their graves with a fresh supply of talents. Recognize that you have the right to reach your dreams. Prepare yourself to knock down the walls of resistance and begin your journey into becoming what you are capable of being.

Self-limitation is not a new trait of man. It has existed for all time and will surely continue to plague us in the future. In our search for success, there will be real and imagined barriers. It is our task to distinguish between the two, to eliminate erroneous ideas, and to carefully plan how to overcome the few real barriers we face. Those are the actions that will make our search successful.

Good advice is often ignored and mistakes are often repeated.
It is a wise man who does neither.

Adding Years To Life

Are you interested in living longer? I'm sure every one reading these words will answer with a resounding, "YES"! But, how much thought have you given to how you might actually do this?

Certainly we can acknowledge that the life expectancy of people has risen in the last fifty years. Each decade, we've increased the age simply because our ability to sustain life with equipment and medicine has dramatically improved. But we shouldn't depend on others to do all the work. We should be willing to help ourselves. Here are the core elements that we can control and the major factors cited as causes for a shortened life span.

The National Center for Disease Control has cited drinking, smoking, stress, diet, and just plain hard living as the major contributors to a shorter life span. Each year, thousands of lives are lost because of these factors. What is important to note is that all are under our control. Only a small percentage of all deaths are due to inadequate health care. The majority of mortality cases are still due to unhealthy behaviors or life-style. In other words, we are killing ourselves at a more rapid rate than diseases are killing us. When we add the increasing number of homicides to this list, the statistics become alarming.

Change can only come about when a willingness to do so is initiated. When one measures the consumption of tobacco products, alcohol and narcotic drugs, it is frightening. The rage to consume is fueled by the eternal optimism that "the other guy will die from these activities, not me." We tell ourselves that we can change anytime we want to. Yes, some abuse themselves and live long lives but they are the exception rather than the rule. Millions are addicted to one form or other of these drugs. They are hooked on a habit that every time it is practiced, takes time off their life.

Stress is a silent killer. We don't inhale, digest, or shoot this killer into our veins. But every day millions are affected by this powerful killer. Control of stress begins with our ability to identify the stressors in our life. The goal is not to totally eliminate stress but to minimize the negative effect it has on our body. There are many excellent books, some of which are noted in the bibliography, that are valuable resources to help you cope with stress. As with drug addiction, there is always professional help available.

Concerning food, many of us are literally "eating" our way to the grave. More and more nutritional studies are revealing the gains one can make by a healthy choice of foods. I must admit that everything with a great taste somehow makes it to the "no no" list. Sometimes it's down right discouraging. However, when I reach sensible thinking levels, I realize that what tastes good isn't always good for me. If adding years to your life is important, watching food intake is a major step in the right direction.

I am greatly saddened by the rising number of murders in this country and, for that matter, around the world. We almost seem to have lost control. We appear to be hell-bent on self-destruction. What drives a person to kill? Anger? Hatred? Revenge? Greed? Insanity? Jealously? Fear? Lust for power? That's a pretty powerful list to use to answer the question. But the one factor that can defuse all of them is concern for the welfare of others.

When we place concern for the welfare of others as our guiding principle, is almost impossible for murder to occur. Violence in the streets could be stopped if all humans embraced this idea. The daily senseless killings all in the name of "getting respect" is frightening. Society is reflecting a serious deficiency in human nature. We must turn this trend around and one of the first steps is for everyone to care for others.

Perhaps your role might be to see what you can do in your relationship with others that can eliminate these causes. Who knows how influential you might be? Who knows what life your actions might save?

Spend time examining your lifestyle and the habits that are eliminating years from your life. Spend time reflecting on what role you might play to improve circumstances for others. Removing destructive habits from our lifestyle and society is in our best interest.

Failure is more often caused by a lack of will than it is by a lack of knowledge.

Just One More Time

One of my favorite books is *Think and Grow Rich* by Napoleon Hill. It is the first self-help book that I read and it has made a lasting impression on me.

In this great classic, Hill says that, *"The starting point of all achievement is desire."* Truer words were never spoken. We must first want the achievement before it can become reality. Strong desire helps build the persistence we need to complete a task. Often, this is the only factor that will guarantee success.

If we desire something strongly enough, we can develop the persistence to achieve that desire. Permit me to share a personal story.

In 1969, I decided to make my first attempt at public office. I was young and politically inexperienced. Seeking to become the next Commissioner of Streets and Parks, I plunged forward into the campaign with no funds or organization. I thought all you needed were the best qualifications and people would support you. What a lesson I learned.

With one loss under my belt, I decided to run for mayor in the next election. If I was going to lead, why not start at the top? Learning some lessons from my first election, I campaigned vigorously. But in spite of my efforts, I failed to achieve my goal. The experience left me wondering what I would have to do to get elected to public office. It tested the level of desire I had for serving.

Four years went by and I got the fever once again. This time, I was seeking a position as a member of the city council. Certainly, I had gained enough information to win this time. But alas, it was not to be. For the third time in eight years, I was a defeated candidate.

In the summer of 1982, I qualified for a seat on our local public school board. As a former teacher, I was attracted to service on the school board. But I had promised to get out of politics after my last defeat. How could I go back on my word to my family? Hesitating until the last hour, I called to see who had qualified. When I learned the incumbent had no opposition, I hurried to the court house and paid my qualifying fee.

It was a difficult time. Qualifying caused strains in my family. As I reflect on that time, it was as if I was driven to do this. I can offer no other reason except I had to do it. My desire to serve and be elected to public office was the strongest it had ever been. I knew I could win and was determined to do so.

In typical south Louisiana political style, the campaign was heated. By far, this was the most difficult and taxing campaign I had ever faced. I persisted, armed with the desire to serve and the belief that I could win.

Election night, after the votes were in, I was defeated for the fourth consecutive time. This time the margin was only eighty-eight votes. But in my mind, something was wrong. I had worked too hard to lose. The vote in every precinct was almost exactly as I had envisioned except for one. In that precinct, I was the loser. That was not as I had predicted.

A business trip was to take me out of town on the day the voting machines were to be opened. I wanted to be there when the machines were opened. I just knew there was an error in the vote count. I asked a friend to be there in my place and to have a certain voting machine opened first.

On Monday, he did exactly as I instructed him. When the machine was opened, my belief was verified. The total votes had been improperly recorded. I had an extra one hundred votes. Instead of losing by eighty-eight votes, the extra one hundred now made me a victor by *twelve votes!* After a few days of agony, the official vote was verified and I maintained my twelve-vote victory.

What was the difference in this campaign? As I reflect on that question, I keep coming back to the same answer. My desire to win and belief that I could was the difference. Other factors played an important part, but believing I could win and wanting to win were the major factors that made winning a reality.

Is there something in your life that has eluded you? With a strong desire to achieve anything you want, you can. The only qualifier is that the desire be strong enough. You might experience temporary failures just as I did, but with persistence you will triumph. Don't overlook the power of your desire and your persistence. They are your best friends in hard times.

Why not commit today to the achievement of that elusive goal? Build your desire to a fever pitch and persist no matter what obstacle gets in your way. With strong desire and a clear vision of what you want, you will overcome obstacles and eventually win. That's the way it works.

Success is a search. Isn't it time you start looking?

Action steps
to
success

1. List places in your life where you could temper your use of power and change it to a more positive force. Explain how you will accomplish the change.

2. What performance could you improve that would make you a more valuable employee, a more caring friend, or a better spouse?

3. Develop your own thirteen-week plan for improving your character. Commit to a one-year application.

4. What barriers have you established that are holding back your potential? What changes could you implement to tear down those barriers?

5. What aspects of your life could stand a little more self-discipline? Establish an action plan to improve.

6. Keep a diary of the food you eat for the next month. Seek professional help to advise you on any improvements.

7. Commit to the achievement of that elusive goal in your life.

Notes & thoughts for action.....

Part V

School Is Never Out

Key Points:

1. Reading is food for the brain.
2. Conduct a personal audit with questions.
3. Don't reinvent the wheel.
4. Life is an eternal teacher.
5. Keep an open mind.
6. Learn from the experience of others.
7. Keep a focus on God.
8. Reading can provide inspiration.
9. Reflect on daily activities.
10. Youngsters can learn from elders.

Never let a day go by without reflection on the activities you've completed or attempted to complete. Use this opportunity as a way to improve your performance tomorrow.

Pretend You're The IRS

If you want to learn more about yourself, the best method is through the use of the questioning technique. I've begun your task by providing the following questions. They are not all encompassing. But they are a start and can serve as a stimulus to generate additional questions. I encourage you to spend time to thoroughly answer each question and to add many more to the list.

Pretend you are the IRS and conduct the most thorough audit ever. It will be a tremendous help as you continue with your search for success.

Conduct a personal audit of your life

1. *What are my marketable skills?*
2. *What can I do better than most other people?*
3. *What have I done particularly well in the past?*
4. *What are my unique talents and abilities?*
5. *What do I enjoy doing?*
6. *In what areas of work do I get the best results?*
7. *If I could do any job at all, anywhere, what would it be?*
8. *How would I describe my ideal job? Ideal lifestyle?*
9. *What have others described as strong points in my character?*

10. *What makes me happy?*
11. *What am I proudest for having accomplished so far in my life?*
12. *What haven't I done that I'd like to do before I die?*
13. *Am I satisfied with my current lifestyle? Income? Achievements?*
14. *What is my personal and professional growth plan?*
15. *What specialized knowledge do I possess?*
16. *What knowledge do I lack that is holding me from reaching my potential?*
17. *What roles do I play? (i.e. father, mother, husband, wife, engineer, writer, welder, secretary, etc.)*
18. *What is the most important principle upon which I base my life?*
19. *Is what I am now doing compatible with this principle?*
20. *Who are the most important people in my life?*
21. *How much time do I spend interacting with these people?*
22. *Is my life balanced?*
23. *If I had unlimited time and resources, what would I do?*
24. *Why am I not doing this now?*
25. *Have I ever taken the time to write goals?*
26. *What is my purpose in life?*
27. *What things have I done in my life that did not make me proud? Why do I feel this way?*
28. *Can I forgive myself and move on with my life?*
29. *Is my lifestyle healthy? (food, exercise, balance, habits, etc.)*
30. *Am I financially secure? If not, what will I do to build that security?*
31. *Am I ready to change to become the "best me" I that can be?*

A person who does not read is no better off than one who cannot read.

The Reading Habit

What do you do when you get hungry? Unless circumstances prevent it, the answer is relatively simple—you seek food. We are so faithful to that habit that we go through the process over a thousand times each year of our life. When the body is in need of food, it's important to eat. The process is essential for continued growth of body cells.

What is the point you ask? If you feed your body over one thousand times each year, how many times per year do you feed your mind? We often forget that our mind also needs its own kind of nourishment. Providing nourishment for our brain helps make the acquisition of food easier. In other words, properly feeding the brain better enables us to earn money to pay for food.

One of the best sources of food for the brain can be found in books. How many books have you read in the last year? Some people never read. Then they wonder why their position in life is static. Other individuals read a book every few days. What specifically should we read? My choice would be books that provide life-changing information. Some call them self-help or inspirational books.

Why read this particular type of book? Allow me to share two stories to illustrate my point.

First, I will use myself as an example. I can tell you **exactly** when my life began to change because of books. The date

110

is June 25, 1978; the book is Napoleon Hill's classic, *Think and Grow Rich*. I had just completed a three-day "Successful Life" course conducted by Ed Forman, CPAE. It was a high energy, fast moving program. As part of the closing exercise, Ed gave each participant a copy of Hill's book. He also gave each of us a list of eleven other books. He strongly encouraged everyone to read the book he had just given us. Then he told us to pick a book from his list, purchase it, and continue doing this until all twelve were read.

By reading the twelve books Ed suggested, my life changed dramatically. These books provided a motivating message and hooked me on the reading habit. Their powerful messages became the keys that opened the doors to a new direction for my life. I changed my outlook on life.

At the peak of my reading habit, I read two books a week. I read at this pace for eighteen months. That was the most incredible growth period of my life. While I've not kept that pace, my current readings are about twenty-five books per year.

Without a doubt, I can attest to the influence books have had on my life. I would go so far as to say that they are the major factor for virtually every success I've experienced since that day in June. This book would never have become a reality had it not been for my reading habit. I don't need convincing on the power of written words!

If you still doubt, let me give you another example. One of America's most famous entertainers attributes the beginning of her career to one particular book. She was a homemaker with five kids and a $50 per week part-time job as a copywriter. She didn't know any people in show business or anything about show business. She lacked the ability to see how she could ever fulfill her dream of being an entertainer.

Her husband recognized that she had talent but she resisted his encouragement for two years before she finally made an attempt at show business. Not until she read Claude Bristol's, *The Magic of Thinking Big,* did she have the courage to try show business. She read and she believed! She maintains that this book showed her how to believe in herself and how to set goals to get what you want from life. It showed her how to apply persistence and never take no for an answer. The words from this powerful book helped her develop a new way of thinking and doing. It focused on *believing in yourself!*

Because of her new belief system and dedication to her goal, she rose to become world famous although she didn't go on stage until she was thirty-seven years old. Who is this lady? None other than Phyllis Diller, the high priestess of the ridiculous.

There are countless others whose life was changed by the written word. What about you? Have you experienced the difference? If books have not yet made a difference for you, why not begin by purchasing one from the list at the end of this book. It is a decision you will not regret and one that will help you on your search for success. *Happy reading!*

112

Your experiences provide valuable lessons. Study them to avoid repeating costly mistakes.

Learning From Others

If I wanted to become a failure, I would seek advice from persons who never succeeded. If I wanted to succeed in all things, I would look for those who are succeeding and do as they have done.

There is great significance in that statement. Letting the wisdom of these words sink in can be a magnificent revelation. They reinforce a message we often forget. How many times have you engaged in an activity and spent countless, fruitless hours attempting to complete the task only to end up unsuccessful? How often could you have been successful if you had only looked around for the lessons life offers?

We don't have time to constantly reinvent the wheel. Someone already did that and our job is to simply use the invention as best we can to complete a life activity. By taking advantage of what other people have already done, we can multiply our effectiveness and achievements. Doesn't that sound like a good idea to you?

What is the reality? Every day we can find examples of people ignoring what history teaches. We seem doomed to repeat failure. One such lesson is constantly forgotten. It's the lesson about the free lunch. By this I mean seeking something without exerting any effort. We have all seen government programs, designed with the best intentions, eventually prove unworkable because the core value is the free lunch concept.

Something for nothing is exactly that—nothing! Recipients eventually move from expectation to demand. They continue to ask for more while doing less. We forget the fish story—feed a man a fish and you only provide food for that day. Teach a man how to fish and you feed him for a lifetime. Officials legislate without accountability and responsibility. That is a recipe for failure.

How many have ventured into new businesses without ever looking at the success techniques people before them have used in similar circumstances. Taking advantage of what others have learned could save time and money and ultimately be the difference between success and failure.

Within the National Speakers Association, we have a unique practice that is a positive illustration of learning from others. It is known as our Mentor Program. Even though we are competitors for the opportunities available within our industry, we also believe that if we can make our competitors better, the value of and demand for our services will increase.

We have established a very successful mentor program in our New Orleans NSA chapter. An experienced speaker is paired with a person wishing to develop a career as a professional speaker. Through a structured process, mentor and mentee get together at regular intervals to plan the mentee's career. No secrets exist. Each mentor is genuinely interested in the progress of his or her mentee and willingly shares information about the speaking business. This one-on-one mentoring shortens the learning curve and helps jump start the beginning speaker.

The program established in New Orleans has proved to be so successful that our model is being used by all chapters within NSA. Mentoring is a proven method where learning from others can produce dramatic results.

114

Every generation seems determined to forge its own way and, in the process, ignore the lessons of the past. Youngsters don't want to listen to the experience of their parents. They want to make their own mistakes. Fortunately, most wake up in later years and discover how much wisdom time had bestowed on their parents. It is unfortunate, however, that we spend so much of our youth ignoring parental experience.

What is the answer? It helps if you move through life with an inquisitive and open mind, with a mind working like a sponge. It helps if you absorb the lessons life offers. Life is an eternal teacher and it is our roll to be the model student. Pay attention to what life offers and you'll end up an honor student.

Few things in life are as valuable as the experience of others. We don't have enough time in our journey for success to repeat worthless experiences. By paying attention to what has happened in the past and to what is happening right now, we shorten the trip to maximum potential. Learn the lessons that are all around us. If we learn more than the average person, we will quickly become above average!

Other people's experience is an important component of your search for success. Don't let this resource go untapped. Using it can really shorten the trip!

Place your faith in God. He is the one who makes all things possible.

Finding Yourself

During a routine review of my library, I came across a great book written by Rollo May entitled, *Man's Search for Meaning.* As I previewed titles for ideas, May's book grabbed me. The words began to remind me of the struggle we all undergo in our pursuit of life. Just when we appear to be reaching a level of satisfaction, some event makes us realize that the journey into understanding ourselves is still unfulfilled.

What makes us what we are? That's not an easy question to answer. We are such complex beings. Many go through their entire lives never getting a satisfying answer to that question. As I've pondered the question, I am drawn to my thoughts as the most powerful influence. We are endowed with a magnificent machine known as the human body. All the activities that take place within our body are governed by the ultramagnificent portion of this creation—the mind!

Studying the magnificence of the human mind can only lead us to the belief that some greater power than us is responsible for its creation. The mind cannot be the work of humans. Use your gift to develop a deeper understanding about yourself.

Our mind can soar in a thousand directions. It's hard work to keep it on track. To keep our sight on the pot of gold at the end of our rainbow does not come easily. It's a discipline that we must constantly strive to keep in place. By keeping a focus on what we want rather than on what we don't want, we can direct the mind to work in our best interest.

116

In today's society we seem to have more and more people who are searching to find themselves. Their lives appear to be an aimless journey with no real purpose. Discovery seems difficult and distant. However, this search for self-discovery has been going on for all times. You may recall the biblical story of the son of a wealthy man who asked his father to give him his share of the estate. He took his share, wasted it on fast living and fast women. Broke, desperate for his next bite of food, he swallowed his pride and went back to his father. Upon his arrival, his father celebrated his return. His lost son had returned. He had finally discovered his real purpose.

That well known biblical story leads me to my final point. When all else fails, go back to your beginnings. Return to the entity responsible for your existence. I'm convinced that humans need a clear belief in God to enable them to find their purpose. Often we distance ourselves from our Creator and claim independence much like the wayward son. But how many times have you seen hardened disbelievers fall back to Him in their hour of need.

Peace and strength of character, in my experience, are synonymous with a strong faith. You know many examples that fortify that belief. I firmly believe that sharing your faith with your God makes understanding ourselves easier to handle.

Are you where you want to be at this point in your life? Have you gained sufficient insight to really know who you are and what is your purpose in the grand scheme of life? The answer to these questions is more easily achieved with a firm faith in God. All things are possible through Him.

Placing unwavering faith in your Creator is the best way to release the abilities you possess. He will free your mind and grant you the wisdom to answer the question, "Who am I?"

Action steps

to

success

1. Complete the personal audit questions beginning on page 107.

2. During the next year, commit to purchasing and reading twelve books from the reading list in Part X.

3. Make a list of all the people you would like to know better. Devise an action plan to meet them in the next twelve months.

4. What new information would you like to learn in the next year? Are there seminars, books, or individuals who can help you? Develop an action plan to help you gather the information.

5. What lessons on life have you learned from your parents? Consider the positive and negative aspects of this question. (This is not to fix blame).

6. If you read a book that makes a difference in your life, please take the time to write me about how it has affected your life. I would be pleased to share your story with others.

Notes & thoughts
for action.....

Part VI

Develop
A
Daily Structure

Key Points:

1. Rise early.
2. Give thanks.
3. Feed your mind.
4. Meditate on occasion.
5. Reflect and resolve.
6. Time is life.
7. Define core values.
8. Analyze your time patterns.
9. Establish a mission statement.
10. Develop written goals.

The best path is not always the easiest to follow.

A Good Way To Start The Day

The first few minutes of your day set the tone for the rest of your waking hours. What you do in the first half hour after you arise is probably the most important activity for that day.

Stop for a minute and recall what you did first this morning. Perhaps you began by reading a book. Perhaps, when the alarm rang, you simply turned it off and rolled over to catch a few more winks. Perhaps you bounced out of bed seconds after the alarm and greeted the day with a smile and lots of enthusiasm for what the day can bring.

I want to share techniques that I've practiced for years. They've never failed to start me off right, and I believe they can work the same way for you.

1. *Rise early.* Begin your day at least two hours before you need to be at work. When I say this to audiences, I usually follow it with the comment, "Now I know that I've lost some of you right now." That statement always draws a chuckle because people understand that most don't want to rise early. I didn't promise it would be easy, I only promised that it worked.

2. *Give thanks for the privilege of living one more day.* That can take the form of a personal prayer or a simple acknowledgment. In part IX, I've provided a prayer that you might read or use as a model to construct your own thank you statement. Anytime you forget the privilege of living one more day, stop and think about the alternative!

3. Follow your thank you statement with this phrase: "It's going to be a great day today!" It's best if you say the words out loud with great enthusiasm. At first, this may seem awkward. But continue the practice and soon you will find yourself acting like a cheerleader at a football game. I've had audiences try this exercise. I never cease to marvel at how much the spirit rises throughout the crowd when they repeat those words in an enthusiastic fashion.

4. The next step is to immediately *smile*. A smile following the great-day statement has an amazing calming effect. Because it's physiologically impossible to feel bad with a smile on your face, you get an immediate lift by exercising some facial muscles. I make numerous references to smiling throughout this book because I'm a great believer in the positive results smiling can produce.

If you want to test this theory, try this. The next time you hear the phone ring, put a great big smile on your face *before* you pick up the receiver. The energy level in your greeting will rise, your caller will sense your energy, and the conversation will open on a positive note. This is particularly effective in a work setting when speaking to customers.

I use this technique when I market my speaking services. I don't like to make cold calls. When I am using this process to make contacts, I start with a smile. It eases the tension and I do a much better job of introducing myself and my services.

5. Before you feed your body, *feed your mind.* It's very important that you provide the right nutrition. Spend between fifteen and thirty minutes reading some inspirational message. You might choose the Bible or a good self-help book. Pay particular attention to the message you read and look for ways to incorporate those ideas into your daily activities. Proper feeding of your mind is an important dietary practice.

6. At least three days a week, engage in some form of exercise. Walking, jogging, or aerobic exercises are good choices. Be sure to consult your doctor before you begin any vigorous exercise program. That is even more important if you've had an inactive lifestyle for some time.

7. An added feature for step six is to listen to inspirational tapes while you exercise. It's a neat way to build your body and mind at the same time. If you don't wish to do this activity while exercising, try listening to tapes in your car as you commute to work.

8. Occasionally, rather than spending time reading, you may simply want to find a quiet spot in the house and meditate. Sitting quietly and letting your mind focus on things that are important in your life is very therapeutic. Don't move. Don't listen to the radio or watch TV. Just sit silently and let thoughts enter your mind. If you have a major obstacle facing you at this time, try the power of silence. It works!

9. Another alternative to reading is to spend time thinking about your goals. Write your ideas. List possible solutions to your problems. Brainstorm for every possible clue and solution. In a quiet environment, your mind quickly becomes a reservoir of ideas.

10. Eat a good breakfast, dress, and go to work with a fresh mind and an enthusiastic attitude.

Now that you've set the proper tone for starting the day, what can you do to maintain the momentum? Go through your day and keep a positive outlook. Focus on what can be. Avoid negative ideas and negative people. Keeping your attitude right makes your day go right.

About noon, take a few minutes to relax in a quiet spot. Just calm down and stop working your brain. Eat a light lunch and mentally prepare for the afternoon's activities.

126

As you continue with your daily activities, take time to evaluate how well you're doing. Are you staying on the course you set? Are you achieving your goals? Before you finish this portion of the work day, spend a few minutes thinking and planning tomorrow's activities. Then you can leave work confident that tomorrow is properly organized and ready for a jump start when you hit the door.

At the end of the day, reflect on your entire list of activities. Compliment yourself for what you did, giving thanks for the good things that happened. Resolve to improve on any poor performance and avoid making the same mistakes tomorrow. Go to bed confident that you've done your best and have earned the right to a good night's sleep.

Keep your life in balance. Don't make it all play or all work. Mix the two and blend your activities with time for family. You now have a formula for starting and completing your day in a positive fashion.

Thomas Edison once said, *"It is astonishing what an effort it seems to be for many people to put their brains definitely and systematically to work. They seem to insist on someone else doing their thinking for them."* Realize that you have control of your thinking every minute of the day. By resolving to begin your day with the proper thinking process, you will experience life like few ever experience it and make your search for success a most enjoyable journey.

Using time wisely is a smart way to live your life.

Moments Of Life

Time is life! The significance of this short three-word sentence escapes many. When you are able to put this thought into perspective, your life takes on new meaning. No one would think of willfully wasting his or her life. It is too precious. But we willfully waste time never realizing that, simultaneously, we are wasting life.

How should we use our time so that it is most beneficial to us? How can we make the best use of our time every moment of the day? I believe the answer is a three-tiered approach. First, we must clearly define our core values. Next, using this information, we define our mission or purpose in life. Finally, we develop goals focused around our mission and values. These goals then become the game plan for using our time in the most effective manner.

Getting control of your life begins by gaining an awareness of how you are using your time. Most people believe they can easily recall last week's activities. In reality, much of what we do cannot be easily remembered. Only by planning our activities and recording this plan in some type of daily organizer can we *really* know how our time is spent each day. By focusing on the activities we do, we can analyze these activities and better determine if they are moving us in the direction we want to go. If you don't currently have the habit of writing your daily activities, I strongly encourage you to begin the process. There are many types of planners available. Use one.

128

The only moment we control is NOW! By taking control of this moment, we can control where we will be the next moment. Doing the right things NOW ensures us that the right things are done later. Remember that yesterday is a canceled check and tomorrow is a promissory note. Only today is legal tender, so spend it wisely.

The first step to capture and control the moments of time is to engage in serious reflection, writing down all your important core beliefs and values. I must tell you that this step is time consuming and difficult. Good things take time and lots of energy, but the payoff is well worth the effort. Complete this exercise alone in a quiet place. Solitude and quietness work.

Once you develop your list, identify the top ten items. With a little further scrutiny, narrow the list to your top five. Take the final five and rank them one through five. **What an important accomplishment that will be!** I assure you, completing this step separates you from most people on earth. Most people see this exercise as too much work so they never convince themselves to complete it.

If you are a bit courageous, ask your family and friends (an adversary or two might also be revealing) to describe you in one-word statements. Sometimes we have a blind side that only others can see. Be open to these comments and receptive to the thoughts shared. It takes a thick skin to constructively work this process. This exercise is revealing as well as rewarding!

Check how your top five values agree with the one-word descriptions you've received. Resolve any conflict that surfaces in your mind. It's important that you become comfortable with how you perceive yourself and how others view you. This last part is a bit risky, but the value of the information gained is well worth the risk. Life is not an isolated venture. We need others and we need their feedback on our behavior if we are to grow.

To illustrate the point on values and further explain this process, I've listed the top five values I strive to follow when making personal and business decisions. It took many years to develop this list. Now that they are visible to me, I can more readily use them to help me refocus whenever I get off course.

1. Model the teachings of Jesus Christ.
2. Family.
3. Integrity in all decisions.
4. Service to others.
5. Excellence.

Why not take some time today to begin focusing on your list. Dedicate whatever time you need to complete this step. It is a necessary step that must be completed before you can start working on the second part of this process.

Once you've clearly identified your top five values, you are ready to move to step two. Using the value list and your descriptors, construct a mission statement. This is an accurate description of what you see as your purpose in life, the reason you are here on earth. Make it simple and clear, easily understood by anyone who might read it. The only rule to remember is that it must be something you can stand behind no matter who challenges your mission. It must be something you can live and breathe every waking moment. It must be something that you dream about day and night. It must be your passion!

Here is the mission statement for my speaking and consulting business: It is simple and direct.

To build an awareness within people of their potential by helping them turn knowledge into results.

130

This mission provides a focus as I develop keynotes, workshops, seminars, or consulting opportunities. It was also the guiding principle as I wrote this book.

The next step is to determine what goals you will need to accomplish your mission. Your goals should be in complete harmony with your values. If they are not harmonious with your values, there will be an internal conflict that will kill your desire to achieve the goals.

Using the following step-by-step process, develop your goals:

1. *You must have a strong desire to achieve the goals.* You will never achieve anything of worth that is half-heartedly desired. You must go to bed thinking about your goals and wake up anxious to continue your journey of accomplishment.

2. *You must have unshakable belief that you can achieve your goals. Make them believable, realistic, yet challenging.* When President John F. Kennedy set a goal to put a man on the moon, he believed it was possible. He helped others believe that it was realistic in spite of the tremendous challenges it presented to the members of the space program.

3. *Write your goals.* Don't rely on your memory. There is a strong reinforcement provided when you can read your thoughts. Some proponents of goal-setting recommend that you take a few minutes each morning to review your goals. During this time, write them on a piece of paper. The act of writing and reviewing goals each day is a constant reminder of your commitment.

4. *List the benefits you will derive from the accomplishment of your goals.* A good salesman knows that it's the benefits that sell. Identifying what you will gain by the achievement of your goals keeps your motivation level high. Benefits really translate into mini-motivators.

5. *Determine where you are compared to where you say you want to be in your goal statement.* Identifying the gap makes setting your action steps an easier process. This step is an ideal place to practice the self-competition I discussed earlier. In the quality process, this step is known as benchmarking. You establish where you want to be and direct all daily efforts towards reaching the benchmark.

6. *Identify the obstacles that stand between your current position and where you want to be.* This step helps you anticipate the unexpected and shortens the attainment time. As I sought election to public office, I was faced with several obstacles. I had to build voter confidence in my ability to serve. I had to organize a campaign, raise money to finance the campaign and solicit campaign volunteers. Ads, signs and handouts had to be printed and distributed throughout the district. Voters expected a visit in their home. Time had to be allocated to walk the miles of my district. On election day, I had to be sure my voters turned out. And the list goes on and on. But I believe you get the point. Detail each step. The more detail the better.

7. *Determine what knowledge you must gain to help you achieve the goals.* If you have a strong desire to sail around the world, it would be a good idea to learn, and master, the principles of navigation before you started the journey. Failing to do this would be disastrous.

8. *Identify resources that could help you accomplish your goals.* There are individuals and organizations who have knowledge and abilities that will speed the accomplishment of your goals. Nurture these synergistic relationships. In the speaking business, my peers and friends who speak professionally are an excellent resource. Building a network of individuals who understand your needs and possess knowledge on how those needs can be met is essential.

132

9. *Write detailed action steps under each goal.* This process enables you to identify and prioritize your daily activities. Review each of the steps you've written to see if they have a natural sequence to them. The sequence you want is smooth, selective and straight-forward. The more exact you can write your action steps, the less time you will waste. So be precise.

10. *Revise and adjust your course.* Spend a few minutes each day to evaluate your performance. If events didn't go as planned, make adjustments. Airline pilots constantly make course corrections as they power their airplanes from one destination to another. Even a degree off course can result in being miles from their destination. Adjust like a good pilot so that you can land safely on the right air strip.

11. *Visualize your success.* The power of the mind to imagine an event is almost limitless. As you use this powerful image maker, experience the emotion you will feel when the goal becomes reality. Seeing and feeling an event is a powerful stimulator.

When my oldest son was in high school, I spoke to the members of his track team and told them the story of Ivory Crockett, a world-class sprinter. Crockett placed a piece of paper in his shoe prior to running a one hundred yard race. He finished in 9.1 seconds. On the paper placed in his shoe were the numbers 9.1! He visualized his success and he achieved his goal.

Leo Sherman was a member of that high school track team. He ran the hurdles. Leo was not an especially fast runner but he had great desire to achieve. One night at a track meet, he achieved a personal best in his race. Everyone was excited for Leo. I went over to congratulate him and he reached in his shoe, pulled out a piece of paper and showed me the numbers. Written on the paper was the *exact* time of his race.

12. *Persist until you succeed.* During World War II, Winston Churchill encouraged the English to resist the Nazi advancement into England. He told them to never give up. In spite of overwhelming odds, they persisted and succeeded in stopping Hitler's army.

Now that I've completed the twelve steps for developing goals, here is the goal I wrote in January 1995 about my book project:

Complete the initial draft of my book by December 31, 1995.

I used the twelve steps just described to help keep me on course and the project was completed by the deadline written. The process works if you do!

Now you are ready to put all this information and effort to good use. You've identified your values, written your mission, and developed goals to support your mission. This final step, a time study, will complete the picture. This process helps provide an orientation from which to start. To understand how you should best use your time to reach your goals, you must understand how you currently use time.

Start on a Monday morning and record everything you do during the day. Don't change your routine or behave any differently than you might if you were not recording your activities. Just continue living life exactly as you have in the past. Every fifteen minutes, write down what you are doing. Continue recording all your activities for at least one entire week. At the end of that time, thoroughly examine your activities and identify the patterns you follow. Determine how much time you spent on each type of activity. Be brutally honest. That's the only way to improve. For best results, repeat the study for a second week.

134

Now you are ready to examine the results of your time study. Compare your activities to your list of values, your mission statement and the goals you've developed. As you do, consider these questions:

1. *How much of my time was spent practicing and adhering to my top five values?*
2. *Are the activities in which I engaged supportive of my mission?*
3. *Will the daily activities I performed help me achieve the goals I've identified as important to me?*

If there is congruency, you are on the right track. If there is no resemblance, you now know why there is such an uneasy feeling dominating your life. We cannot work against our core beliefs and values and maintain a happy lifestyle. That won't work. Like oil and water—they just don't mix.

Completing the process of identifying your values, developing a mission statement that supports your values, and writing goals to accomplish the mission will place you high on the ladder of success. You will now have a reason to get up in the morning. Life will take on a new meaning. Excitement will permeate every aspect of your life. Every day will be a great day!

Action steps
to
success

1. For a fourteen-day period, practice using the suggestions on how to have a good day outlined on pages 123-126.

2. Make a list of all the things that you are putting off doing in your work place, home, with your family, friends, and in your community. Take action on your lists.

3. Commit to finding five extra hours each week to spend on your high priority activities.

4. Complete a time study and develop action steps to improve how you use your time.

5. Make a Victory List (all the things you are proud to have done in your lifetime). Refer to it when you start feeling like you haven't done much with your life.

6. Identify your top five values. Construct a mission statement using these values as your guiding principles. From the mission statement, write at least three goals you are willing to commit to accomplishing within the next twelve months.

Notes & thoughts
for action.....

Part VII

Build People Bridges

Key Points:

1. Be nice to everyone.
2. Be sensitive to the feelings of others.
3. Help those who need help.
4. Don't gossip.
5. Be interested in people.
6. Remember names.
7. Make people feel important.
8. Don't dominate a conversation.
9. The customer is boss.
10. Admit when you are wrong.
11. Measure customer satisfaction.
12. Trust your mate.
13. Form a mutual admiration society.
14. Allow for differences.
15. Build compatibility and companionship.

Life offers many rewards. None is greater than extending a kindness to someone with no expectation of personal gain from the act.

The Golden Gift

During most of the years I attended elementary school, a major soft drink company would give students an ink blotter, a ruler, and a bright red pencil. Every student looked forward to getting these gifts. The gifts were especially important to those of us whose parents didn't have the money to buy such items. Even after fifty years, I still appreciate the gesture.

Certainly, the gifts were an effective tool to promote their business. I'm sure the payoff was many times the value of the gift. While giving had a certain self-serving side, there was also a benefit to each recipient. One particular gift, the ruler, probably had the greatest impact on students. It was painted with a golden finish and the black lettering added a tone of richness that made you proud to be the owner. A simple message was embossed on the ruler, "*Do unto others as you would have them do unto you.*"

This company wanted to teach youngsters one of the most important ideas in human relations. Teachers made sure we practiced this message. Our parents were also reinforces of this principle. Little by little, we learned the significance of the Golden Rule. I'm thankful for being taught this rule. It was one of the greatest lessons of my life. I believe I am still bene-fiting from this lesson today.

142

Imagine with me if you will what the world would be like today if everyone adhered to that simple rule. How could there ever be war? How could hatred exist? How could people kill? Yes, the world would be a much better place if everyone treated others as they wished to be treated. There would be no prejudice, no crimes, no mistreatment of human life. What a wonderful thought!

By following the Golden Rule, we place value on human life—value on the life of others as well as our own. We acknowledge that we cannot exist alone. We need other people to help us reach our destination.

If you doubt the validity of what I'm saying, please try this experiment for the next thirty days. Go out of your way to be as nice as possible to everyone you meet. Don't get mad. Be pleasant, smile a lot, and treat others as you would want to be treated. I can guarantee that this will be an unforgettable experience. These encounters will make a real difference on the way you view the world.

It would be very interesting to hear how your thirty-day experiment went. If you are willing to share those events with me, I just might use your example in a future book, article or presentation.

By adopting the Golden Rule, you will take a giant step toward completing your search for success.

You won't get a chance to relive your life, so don't miss an opportunity to extend a kindness to all you meet.

You Only Pass Through Once

In the realm of eternity, our lives are smaller than one grain of sand on all the beaches of the world. But, even in this short period of time, we are charged with making our own contribution. I could produce a long list of worthy activities to pursue but I'd rather concentrate on four simple acts. Each can be implemented with little or no money. Yet, their impact on our life and character is priceless.

1. *Avoid being a gossip.* Let's face it, we love to talk about others. Playing put-down seems to be a favorite pastime. In reality, playing this game diminishes our self-worth. By attempting to place ourselves above others, we inadvertently sink in credibility.

American historian George Bancroft, in *The International Dictionary of Thought,* says, *"Truth is not exciting enough for those who depend upon the characters and lives of their neighbors for all their amusement."* Bancroft understood the motivation of gossip.

Show kindness to others by avoiding the practice of gossiping. Don't build your reputation by tearing down the reputation of others. That is not a character building exercise. It is better to say nothing than to talk about others in a demeaning way.

2. *Be sensitive to the feeling of others.* There is an old song entitled, "You Always Hurt the One You Love." Sometimes we say things to people we love that pierce their heart. The harshness of our words, the viciousness of our actions are aimed at hurting. When all is said and done, we are regretful. But the damage is done. In strong relationships, people can move on and, in many cases, the relationship grows stronger.

Where the relationship is fragile, this type of confrontation leads to disastrous results. By raising our antenna and becoming more sensitive to the weight our actions and words carry, we can dramatically reduce the potential to hurt the feelings of others. Think before you speak or act. Pause just a minute before you respond. Always care what effect your actions have on others.

3. *Do something for someone expecting nothing in return.* If you really want to experience a good feeling, extend a helping hand to someone just because they need help. Don't do it for any self-serving reason. Do it because it's the right thing. Providing food for a hungry family; making a toy for a child at Christmas; donating money to a worthy cause—these are pure acts of kindness. Doing such things for people gives you a high no drug could ever match.

4. *Learn to forgive.* Is there anyone in your life right now that you truly don't like? Take out a piece of paper and write the reason why you don't like them. Be as clear and concise as you can. Now here is the hard part. Vividly picture that person. When you have a clear vision of their face, say these words: **"I LOVE YOU."** To maximize the experience and assure success, add all the emotion and feeling you can muster as you speak. If you successfully raise the right emotion, you should literally feel the hate draining from your body.

This is a very powerful exercise. I remember doing this during a particularly tense political relationship. My chest was hurting from the tension. I soon realized that I could not change this person but that I did have control over changing myself. With all the emotion I could muster, I pictured his face and said, "*I Love You.*" Immediately, I felt huge burden lifted from my shoulders. Never again did I experience the tension. I don't have to be sold on the merits of this technique. It works!

5. *Be a friend.* One of the most memorable displays of friendship was between Brian Piccolo and Gale Sayers, running backs for the Chicago Bears. Piccolo knew little about blacks and Sayers had never really established a friendship with a white person. They became roommates and went on to establish one of the strongest friendships in the ranks of professional football.

The year Gale Sayers was honored as the recipient of the George S. Halas Award at the Professional Football Writers annual dinner, Piccolo was diagnosed with cancer. In spite of his serious condition, Piccolo had planned to attend the award dinner. The night of the award, Piccolo was confined to his bed and too ill to attend the dinner. In tears, Sayers accepted the award and dedicated it to his friend Brian Piccolo. "*I love Brian Piccolo,*" are the words everyone remembers about his acceptance speech. What a friend we would be if we could unabashedly express our friendship in such strong terms.

We only get one chance at life. Make the trip more fulfilling and pleasurable by extending kindness towards everyone you meet. The result will be a degree of happiness more intense than any scale can measure.

146

Being a friend is the best way to gain friendships.

Getting People To Like You

Life is not a solo act! If we are to experience any kind of success, we need the help of other people. For them to help us, they must like us. How can we get people to like us? Permit me to share six ideas you might try.

First and foremost, for people to like us, we must have a genuine interest in them. We must understand that a person is more interested in themselves than they are in us. So, by showing an interest in other people, you automatically get their attention. Psychologist Alfred Adler wrote, *"It is the individual who is not interested in his fellow men who has the greatest difficulties in life and provides the greatest injury to others. It is from among such individuals that all human failures spring."* Strong words! Think about your relationships. Are they based upon this concept?

The sweetest sound to most people is the sound of their name. It's impressive to meet a person who remembers your name the *second* time you meet. The most easily learned technique to remember a name is to simply listen when you are introduced. Most of us don't give remembering names a high priority. Imagine everyone you meet as your next boss. That's a person you would not forget when first introduced. Repeating the name during your conversation is another technique that helps reinforce your memory. If it is unusual, ask the person to pronounce or even spell it for you. No one is offended when you are making a serious effort to remember who they are.

This brings me to the third point. People will endear themselves to you if you are a good listener. Who is the best conversationalist you know? I guarantee you it's not the person who is a perpetual talker. It will always be the person who listens and lets you talk. If you want to lose friends, talk only about yourself and constantly interrupt conversations with your answer to the issues under discussion. The next time you are at a gathering, practice being a good conversationalist—listen! The results might make it one of the most memorable evenings you've ever experienced.

Endearing people to you in conversations is easily done by letting them talk about topics near and dear to their heart. This fourth point is difficult because we, like most people, would rather speak about our topic of interest. But remember, you're trying to win other people to your side. It's okay to speak about things that interest you but don't let it be the dominant conversation of the evening. At first, this may be very difficult. With a little determination and a desire to win friends, this technique will bring about a win-win event.

A fifth technique to get people to like you is to smile a lot. Aren't the people you like most great smilers? Isn't this one of the key reasons you are attracted to someone? A great smile is an icebreaker. It makes the smiler feel good and it makes the person viewing the smile feel good.

Smiling is a powerful practice. Look in the mirror and practice your smile. Think SMILE all day long. When you greet someone, even a stranger, smile. When you are feeling down, put a smile on your face. When you answer the phone, smile before you say a word. When you awaken in the morning, smile even if you have to push your cheeks up with your fingers. Try these activities. They cost nothing to give but are priceless to the receiver.

148

One of the greatest techniques for winning friends is to make people feel important. This feeling is the strongest non-biological urge of humans. Everyone has it. Everyone needs it. We all want to be appreciated. Actually, by practicing the first five steps, you automatically achieve this one. Anytime you take an interest in others, smile at lot at people, practice active listening, remember names, and speak in terms of the other person's interest, and you will convey a sense of importance to others. Use every opportunity you have to make people feel important. By appreciating others, they will appreciate you more and your goal of getting people to like you will be reached.

The information in this chapter is so important that I want to review the key points one more time. The six factors that will build friendships are:

1. Have a genuine interest in people.
2. Remember names.
3. Listen.
4. Let people talk about their areas of interest.
5. Smile a lot.
6. Make people feel important.

We need people to survive in this world. Ralph Waldo Emerson said is best with this statement: *"The only way to have a friend is to be one."*

Learn how to work well with others. Reread and practice the principles mentioned in this chapter. They work! Their acquisition is a giant step in your search for a successful life.

To improve service to customers, ask them to tell you about their level of satisfaction and ways to improve what you now do.

We Are All In The Customer Service Business

Who is your boss on the job? You're probably thinking about your immediate supervisor or manager. To some degree, you are certainly right. But there is a little trickery in this question. No matter what job you have, there is always a common boss. Your real boss is the customer that allows you to be in business or allows your employer's company to remain in business. Organizations that forget the customer are soon history.

While price is a consideration customers give to the services or products you provide, it's the quality of that service or product that is of primary importance. People will remember service long after they have forgotten the price. Striving to make outstanding customer service your business goal will reap positive results. By improving the life of your customer, you also improve your own well-being.

I'd like to share with you ten rules for good customer service that you can immediately put into practice no matter what your occupation.

1. *Focus on problem identification.* Your business exists because it can solve problems. When you can identify and solve problems for your customers, you earn loyalty.

Take all complaints seriously but not personally. As you work on a solution, be sure that the customer agrees with it. Nothing is accomplished in the eyes of your customer until they are satisfied you've done all you can do to resolve their problem. Respond rapidly and keep your word once an agreement is reached. Follow-through is most important.

2. *Keep accurate records, particularly for quality problems.* Unless you keep good records, repetitive complaints could go unnoticed. By keeping careful records of all conversations with customers, you can more easily identify trends and successfully prevent similar occurrences. The more you know, the more you can do.

3. *Listen! Listen! Listen!* I don't believe I have to say much about this point. Nothing will do you more good than genuinely listening to a customer. Sometimes all they want is a sympathetic ear. Listening also helps you identify the problem faster and bring the whole matter to a successful close more quickly.

4. *Practice empathy and sympathy.* You should always strive to see the complaint through the eyes of your customer. Ask yourself, "How would I like to do business with me?" Treat customers as you would a guest in your home. By taking a genuine interest in their concerns, you build rapport and confidence. This is not always easy but it is the right thing to do.

5. *Smile.* Never underestimate the power of a pleasant smile. It's impossible to be difficult when you are smiling. Likewise, it's hard to stay mad at a smiling face. A genuine smile is an icebreaker.

6. *Be honest and level with a customer when something goes wrong.* Never lie to a customer. Remember that your customer is more interested in what you can do for him than he is in your goods or services.

7. *Never miss an opportunity to express appreciation for your customers' business.* This thought ranges from a cordial hello to a sincere thank you for their business. In between these two points, do all you can to present a positive, polite, and patient attitude.

8. *Don't run down the competition—show the difference.* Nothing is gained by criticizing your competition. Have you ever seen a statue erected to a critic? All you have to do is show how you are different. If you offer more for the same price, you'll get the business.

9. *Periodically measure your customers' satisfaction.* Nothing in life should go unevaluated. There are a variety of tools available from written surveys to conversation. Regardless of the method, do it. Information gained from customer feedback can be invaluable. Use the knowledge gained to make the necessary adjustments to your business, thus ensuring continual customer loyalty.

10. *Show concern for your customer as a person.* This last point is most important. People want to be appreciated and customers are no exception. This is not something you can fake. You must be genuinely interested in their welfare and business. Learn all you can about them, their family, hobbies, health, or any other interest. If you truly care about your customer, they will care for you. Harvey McKay, author of *Swim With the Sharks,* is the master at gathering information. He has sixty-six categories of information he strives to get on every customer. His rolodex files contain over six thousand names. Does Harvey have a successful business? You bet!

If people within an organization don't work together, they cannot make a good product. If a good product isn't made, a good product cannot be sold. If a good product cannot be sold, you don't have a business. Pretty serious thought!

152

Marriage is not something you enter with a half-hearted commitment. It takes a lifetime of work to keep it together.

Make Me A Part Of Your World

Each year the statistics seem to rise: more and more people are filing for divorce. Roughly half of all marriages end up failures. I won't pretend to have all the answers to such a complex issue. What I'd like to pass on to you is what has worked well for my wife and me. We've spent the last thirty-four years together. Have all these years been free of turmoil? Certainly not. But there are methods we've learned that help solidify our relationship. I hope the list proves beneficial to you in your marriage or budding relationship.

1. *Share the same values.* In all the years of our relationship, we have never had a values clash. Raising four children presented many opportunities for disagreement. That never occurred because we supported each other's decisions on discipline. The values we sought to incorporate into our children's lives were equally reinforced by both of us. This commonality is one of the strongest bonds we possess and, in my opinion, can be a major source of conflict if vastly different in husband and wife. If you are experiencing relationship difficulties, try sitting down and listing your values. It's a good place to start the healing.

2. *Trust each other.* If trust is missing, your relationship is doomed to failure. A jealous spouse will create conflict. That conflict can grow intense enough that separation may be the only alternative. Few couples are around each other twenty-four hours a day so both partners will have to trust the faithfulness of the other. If the belief by both partners is rock solid, the likelihood of having a relationship with another person is almost nonexistent. There is something wonderful about a monogamous relationship that is perpetuated by a high degree of trust. It's the ultimate safe-sex practice.

3. *Build compatibility and companionship.* A common reason cited in divorce proceedings is noncompatibility. The truth is, carbon copies of yourself are rare. Besides, that could really be boring. It's inevitable that there will be strong differences between couples. However, building a relationship demands that you work out differences. Each of you needs to be able to do their own thing. What you look for are the opportunities to do things together. Building a relationship takes effort and commitment. It will not just happen. Some compromise may be in order but it should be shared, otherwise resentment can build.

Over the years, my wife and I have built our own special interest activities. She enjoys quilting, I enjoy speaking and writing. She enjoys interior design, I enjoy woodworking. These activities give each of us our own identity. We have built compatibility on the common bond of our children and grandchildren. They are a very important part of our lives and we both enjoy opportunities to be with them. We also both enjoy traveling and exploring new places. We look for opportunities to be individualistic but, at the same time, we have built compatibility on many fronts.

154

4. *Remember all the parts of the wedding vow.* When the marriage vows are said, one part includes the term, *"for better or worse."* There will be times when you will be tested on that phrase. There will be times when you might feel like walking away from the relationship. What keeps you together? The commitment you made to each other. The words fairly well cover the entire spectra and, when taken at face value, provide the glue which bonds your relationship.

"Until death do us part," is another serious part of that commitment. Death is the finality to life on earth—the end—kaput! Remembering that promise means you will sometimes have to do some serious forgiving. We all mess up! Be ready to honor your promise and chances are you will have no difficulty keeping it.

5. *Build sexual compatibility.* Now, this section is not another version of *The Joy of Sex.* Sorry! But I must mention this aspect of a marital relationship. All sex will not be good. Every sexual encounter will not be wanted by both partners. But if you view such encounters as opportunities to express love for your partner, it goes way beyond satisfaction of the physical urge. It may take time to build a comfort level with each other but if the goal is always concern for your mate, you will reach a fulfillment that makes your marital bond stronger and stronger. There will be no need to look to others.

6. *Get together on the finances.* Money problems can be a major source of conflict in a marriage. It is often the major factor in a divorce proceeding. The only way to minimize conflict is to agree upon how finances will be handled. Some compromise is in order but, with a sincere effort, mutual consent can prevail. Working from a budget is the best opinion I can offer. Finances are an important part of a marital relationship, particularly in today's high-cost economy.

7. *Form a mutual admiration society.* If you don't have traits you admire in your partner, the relationship is doomed before it starts. Discover the strengths each of you possesses. Cultivate them. Building support is an important ingredient. Be a cheerleader for your partner. As you help each other grow, the relationship gets stronger and soon it is too strong to ever falter.

8. *Allow for differences.* This may sound contradictory to previous statements. But, no matter how you look at it, men and women are different. They have different physical, mental and emotional needs. Successful marriages allow for those differences. By allowing your spouse to be his or her own person, you simultaneously allow them to open up to change. You cannot remake your spouse. You can only change yourself.

Building a strong marriage takes energy and commitment. Work on the points discussed in this chapter and they will help build solidarity that will last a lifetime. That, my friend, is an important part of your search for the ultimate success story.

Action steps
to
success

1. For the next thirty days, look for ways to implement the principle of the golden rule with everyone you meet.

2. Build an awareness of when you are talking about others in a negative fashion. How might you eliminate this trait from your life?

3. Is there anyone in your life right now that you truly do not like? Attempt to heal this feeling by doing the "I love you" exercise discussed on page 144.

4. How well do you remember names? Incorporate the suggestions from page 146 to help you improve.

5. Identify your customers on the job. This can include fellow workers who use your services or information as well as people who purchase your products. Develop an improvement plan to increase your service to everyone.

6. Develop a self-improvement plan to improve relationship with your spouse or companion based upon the eight points discussed on pages 152-155.

Notes & thoughts for action.....

Part VIII

Success Challenges

Key Points:

1. Don't be content where you are.
2. Develop a take-charge attitude.
3. We impose self-limitations on ourselves.
4. Appreciate the magnificence that surrounds us.
5. Greatness can inspire.
6. Dare to stretch, grow, and conquer fears.
7. Clearly identify your problems.
8. Don't procrastinate.
9. Follow-through gets the job done.
10. As ye sow, so shall ye reap.

No one is programmed to fail. We have the innate skills to fulfill our dreams. What we usually lack is the awareness of our deficiencies and the will to sufficiently use what we have.

Don't Just Be—Become!

How satisfied are you that you have reached your pinnacle of achievement? If you are candid, you will admit that there certainly are greater heights to achieve. Why do we know better, but don't do more? In my search for the answer to that question, I've come to this conclusion. We don't set challenging goals. Some of us don't even bother to set nonchallenging goals. We are content to be. We never think of becoming.

Becoming is hard work! Overcoming the inertia to remain static and nonchanging takes tremendous energy. We fill our minds with self-doubt. We believe we don't deserve to rise above the crowd and separate ourselves from the masses. We do ourselves a tremendous disservice by willingly standing still while the opportunities of the world pass by.

I remember going to an amusement park in New Orleans during my early childhood. This park had a beautiful merry-go-round ride. One feature of the ride was trying to reach out to catch a brass ring. Each rider on the outside row of horses passed by the brass ring holder. As you passed, if you were able to stretch out and hook the ring with your finger, you would receive a free ride. It was a stretch for a young child. It was risky because one could fall off the horse. But the thought of getting that free ride overcame those concerns. Hooking the ring was the all-consuming goal.

164

What about you? Are you on a merry-go-round? Are you content to just go round and round? Or do you risk and stretch to catch the brass ring? The brass ring represents opportunities in life. How many have you caught? How many have you missed? How many have you simply ignored because you were afraid to risk and stretch? Don't focus on the possibility of falling off the horse. Focus on catching the ring.

Life offers all of us lots of brass rings. They don't fall into our hands. We must stretch beyond the feeling of comfort to reach them. But what an exhilarating feeling we get when we can feel our fingers grabbing hold of the ring. What a feeling of accomplishment we have when we know the ring is not going to slip out of our grasp.

As you develop a take-charge attitude in your search for success, don't be content to ride through life without risk, without stretching yourself to the limit of your abilities. Life is good but we must do our share. Concentrate on becoming. Don't just be! It's the only way to truly take charge of your life and reach the successes you truly deserve.

Sometimes it only takes the natural beauty of the world to inspire us.

It's All In Our Point Of View

As I looked out of the airplane window at 30,000 feet on a flight to San Francisco, I was in awe of the majestic beauty before me. The vastness of the horizon's dark blue contrasting with the white velvet cloud formations was an inspiring sight. Below me were tree-covered mountains with their red clay bodies and snow-capped peaks. They make a sharp contrast to the flat plains of the western desert lands.

There is a sense of greatness just to be able to view part of nature's design from such a vantage point. The experience is a tribute to the genius of dedication to a goal—the dream of flying. It began with the Wright brothers who decided to take charge and build their flying machine. They refused to believe cynics who repeatedly told them flying was impossible. Their point of view was different and they moved forward boldly until they conquered their dream.

I liken this view from an airplane seat to the vastness of opportunity that is open to everyone. The only limitations are those we impose on ourselves. In America, we can become what we want to be. It's all in our point of view.

Look around. Opportunities surround us. We only need to prepare ourselves and be ready to act when conditions dictate. Winners think the rewards are worth the sacrifice. Losers believe the price it too great. It's all in our point of view.

166

As I continued my flight, I began to feel a closeness to the Master Architect, the Creator of all this wondrous beauty. The inspiration ignited the fires of motivation, and with this stimulus, the feeling of being able to carry through on dreams emerged. With such internal inspiration, obstacles become stepping stones to success. With such power, impossibilities become possibilities. It's all in your point of view.

In this brief moment of sharing one scene from my life, I hope I've begun to build an awareness of the beauty that is all around you. Such beauty is often taken for granted, yet it can provide a stimulus to change your thinking.

I believe it was the anticipation of getting that view from the top that stimulated Orville and Wilber to dare to fly. I believe that in some way, the beauty of this earth was a factor that brought success to their venture into the airways.

Frank Lloyd Wright, one of the world's greatest architects once said, *"The human race built most nobly when limitations were greatest and, therefore, when most was required of imagination in order to build at all. Limitations seem to have always been the best friends of architecture."*

Wright realized that the miraculous architecture of this earth makes us aware of our own limits. But, at the same time, the majestic beauty can inspire creativity. It is this creativity that has moved the world forward and challenged man to seek greatness. It is also one piece of the formula that can help you complete your search for success.

Those who dare also willingly take the risk to fail.

I Dare You

It was nearly forty years ago when I was first given the "I Dare You" challenge. During my high school graduation ceremony, I received an award from the Danforth Foundation. It was a small book of 134 pages entitled, *I Dare You.*

The little red book was full of challenges. But, as a young man of eighteen, I figured I didn't need to study this message. I was going forth to conquer the world. The last thing I needed was advice from a book.

Eighteen years passed before I sat down and truly read the messages offered by the little red book. How foolish I was to wait so long. How foolish I was not to take advantage of the messages offered. Priceless advice like—

Dare to stretch and become the best me possible.
Dare to grow and broaden my knowledge.
Dare to lift my head above the crowd and be true to myself at all times.
Dare to conquer my fears.
Dare to remain physically and mentally strong.
Dare to maintain a positive attitude and full of energy and enthusiasm.
Dare to overcome the obstacles of the mind and think creatively.
Dare to build the character and personality of a winner.
Dare to build a life of service to others.

168

What great advice! What powerful information that lay untapped for so long. What foolishness to ignore these powerful messages.

Allow me, if you will, to offer you my own "I Dare You" challenges. They are easy to remember because the key words spell out DARE. I hope you will not wait eighteen years to implement them.

The first challenge is centered on the word *discipline*. By discipline I mean being able to do something that you must do even though you do not feel like doing it. It means being able to say "no" when "yes" would be the easy way. Sometimes that may mean risking the loss of friends that want you to act like a loser. Avoiding drugs, excess alcohol, and other activities that ruin your health should be at the top of your "no" list.

Being disciplined can also mean passing up that favorite TV program if you have to study for a test or if important time is needed for family activities. Learning how to use discipline throughout your life will separate you from the masses and make your life a winning experience. *I dare you to make DISCIPLINE a part of your life!*

For the second challenge, I've chosen the word *attitude*. Proper development of a winning attitude is perhaps the most important activity upon which you should concentrate. When you approach life with the right attitude, you gain the respect of teachers, co-workers, family, friends, and foes alike.

The single most important factor that contributes to your success is your attitude. It is more important than your education or job training. Do a check-up from the neck-up. *I dare you to make a POSITIVE ATTITUDE the core of your personality!*

Next, the challenge moves to the word *responsibility.* This word is the central theme of my book. What a critical acquisition. Don't be among the people who go around and blame all their troubles on someone else. They refuse to accept responsibility for their life. Their failure to understand the significance of this fact is the root cause of their troubles. Understanding that WE ARE RESPONSIBLE represents the highest form of knowledge a human can possess. No one else can do it for us. We must do it ourselves and accept full responsibility for our failures just as we want the credit for our successes. *I dare you to be RESPONSIBLE!*

My final challenge is represented by the word *enthusiasm.* Possessing enthusiasm helps make life an exciting journey. You can succeed at almost anything for which you have unlimited enthusiasm. Learning about something new is a way to build enthusiasm. Smiling a little more, raising the excitement in your voice or simply offering an uplifting "thank you" to people makes your enthusiasm grow. Setting meaningful and fulfilling goals builds the fires of enthusiasm into a raging fire of accomplishment. Yes, *I dare you to be ENTHUSIASTIC!*

Life is full of choices. I've offered you four to consider. The payoff for making the right choice is a more productive and enjoyable stay on earth.

The strong take the rocks of life and use them to build a smoother and stronger path to their dream.

Learning To Decide

Have you ever been in a situation where you just didn't know what to do? No matter how hard you tried, making a decision just didn't seem possible. Maybe you're at such a point right now. If you are, here are some proven steps you can use to help solve a problem and make that decision to eliminate it.

The first step is to precisely define the nature of the problem. It's impossible to make a decision about something that is undefined. How often have you tried to solve a problem without a clear definition of the situation? Take time to write, with laser clarity, the dilemma dragging you down. There is something about seeing the words that provides great clarity.

Next, take a piece of paper and begin to list all the possible solutions. Don't limit yourself. Write all ideas, no matter how ridiculous they may seem when first developed. When done with this part, review each item again and begin to weed out all the impractical ideas.

Once you've completed these first two steps, you are ready to get to the heart of the issue. Pick the most likely solution. Before you begin to move forward with your idea, determine all the possible obstacles that might prevent you from carrying out the solution. This is one of the few times that I will encourage you to practice negative thinking. By thinking of every possible bad thing that can occur, you are actually taking a very positive step.

The next step is to gather all the information you can about the problem. The more information you have, the better able you are to make the right decision. So be a good detective.

Now that you've gathered your information, examine all the possibilities and then begin to develop your decision. Many times, this is where procrastination creeps in. We become frozen, afraid that we will chose the wrong path. Don't be afraid to be wrong. If you've gone through each step with your best effort, the odds favor your success. Go ahead and make the decision.

What we've come down to is action. Nothing good can ever happen until action is involved. Sometimes just moving on the problem is enough to ease tensions and stress. Just sitting still only produces more problems.

The final step is to do follow-up on your action. See your decision through until you are sure the job is done. Once you've acted, spend time reflecting and evaluating the results. When done with this step, you've just turned all problems into opportunities and challenges.

Let me illustrate the preceding steps by using an actual problem I might face while running a business. To keep pace with the competition, I need new office equipment but I have limited funds available. The items I need include a computer upgrade, new software, a fax machine, an eight-hundred line with voice mail, a copier, and a LCD projector. I might state the problem this way: How do I finance the purchase of office equipment needed to upgrade my service to clients with only $2000 available?

I begin to make my list of solutions. I could barter my services taking equipment as payment. I could seek a loan using my funds as a down payment. I might check the newspaper ads for used equipment from a bankruptcy sale.

172

I would continue the brainstorm session until I had exhausted all possible avenues of building revenue. I would move further into the process by defining specifications for each piece of equipment. Questions I might ask would include the specifications I am looking for and the applications I need to address. I would study reliability of certain brands. I would talk to people using a brand I might want. I would check on the availability of repair service.

When I've completed gathering information, I am ready to decide on the best option. What I find is that there is very reliable equipment available from a business in my city. Everything I need, including specific brands I want, is carried by this supplier. I find that he is competitive with prices, provides excellent service guarantees, and offers financing free of interest for one year. I can make a nice down payment with some of the cash I have and get all the supplies I need. I take action and make the purchases.

If you have a tendency to be indecisive, why not incorporate these steps into your problem-solving procedure. Always remember that every problem has within it the seeds of its own solution. Most of the time, all you have to do is attack it in a sensible, systematic way and the solution surfaces. That is how to keep your search for success moving in the right direction.

"Oh what shall I do? How will it end?
Decisions, decisions making me bend.
Problems galore, it's so hard to go on.
I know I'll stop, and soon they'll be gone.
But alas, the truth of it all
Is that indecision will be my downfall.
Action, action will rid me of strife
You see, I've decided to take charge of my life!"

If you spend your life thinking about the things you don't want to happen, you'll spend a lifetime doing the things you didn't want to do.

The Forgotten Law Of Life

Up to this point, I've discussed a number of examples of how one could proceed on their search for building a successful life. There is one final point that I want to emphasize even though I touched on it on several occasions in this book. I want to repeat the thought because this idea is probably the most misunderstood, misused law in the universe. It is the law that guides the universe.

On civil or criminal matters, a law is a rule that is binding on those governed by it. It cannot be violated without consequences. If one engages in the act of stealing, one can expect to reap the consequences of the act when caught by the police. (There is also a consequence when you are not caught, but that's another story.)

In the scientific arena, there are laws whose outcome is predictable and accurate given the same set of circumstances. If you fall from the roof of your home, you can expect to hit the ground relatively soon. That's how the law of gravity works.

In life, the forgotten law is also never failing. However, this law is a bit different from the two examples I've just cited. Besides the negative potential, there is a positive side as well.

174

This law has been expressed in a number of ways. The one I prefer is taken from the Bible. In the Bible it says, *"As ye sow, so shall ye reap."* Commentator, author, and master of words, Earl Nightingale, called it the *"Boomerang Principle."* Professional speaker Brian Tracy, CSP, CPAE, simply says, *"Everything Counts."*

I want you to fully appreciate how you can use this law to help you on your journey to success. By carefully structuring your life so that you do the things necessary to get the results you desire, you will ultimately reach your success destination.

The following ten laws are given to you as a reminder of what One greater than us has strongly suggested we follow. Adhering to these laws will provide you with a ticket for the ultimate destination life was intended to provide.

1. *I am the Lord your God, you shall have no strange gods before me.*
2. *You shall not use the name of the Lord, your God in vain.*
3. *Remember to keep holy the Lord's day.*
4. *Honor your father and your mother.*
5. *You shall not kill.*
6. *You shall not commit adultery.*
7. *You shall not steal.*
8. *You shall not bear false witness against your neighbor.*
9. *You shall not covet your neighbor's wife.*
10. *You shall not covet your neighbor's goods.*

Positive use of this never-failing law will produce a joyous and productive lifestyle. The choice is clear. *Do the right things and get the right results. Do the wrong things and get the wrong results.* How magnificently simple!

Action steps
to
success

1. What do you want to become?

2. Beginning tomorrow morning, increase your awareness of your surroundings. Take in the beauty of the land. Learn to appreciate God's creations.

3. Review the dare list on page 167 and accept the challenge each point offers.

4. What are the top three "problems" in your life right now? What obstacles are getting in the way of solving them? Implement the problem solving steps outlined on pages 170-172 to help close out those problems.

5. What decisions do you hate to make? Why? What can you do to be more assertive with your decision process?

6. Examine your decision-making style. What is the basis you typically use to make decisions?

7. In the Bible, God gave us the ten commandments. Reflect on how well your life follows these rules.

Notes & thoughts
for action.....

Part IX

Closing Thoughts

Key Points:

1. Recognize "rut" living.
2. Get close to God.
3. Examine your life.
4. Pray.
5. Find serenity.
6. Build courage.
7. Use wisdom.

Anyone can stay in the rut of mediocrity. It takes a different person to recognize 'rut' living and do something about it.

The Manresa Experience

One of the great joys of my life is the annual retreat I attend at the Manresa House. Since 1991, I've driven the short distance from my home to the beautiful retreat setting along the banks of the Mississippi River. Manresa provides an inspirational setting with hundreds of stately oak trees on the grounds. It is an ideal environment for spiritual renewal. What is unique about the retreat is the vow of silence every participant practices. Here is how it works.

Each Thursday evening at 6:00 pm about one hundred men arrive at Manresa to begin their retreat. After everyone checks in and the evening meal is complete, the first of a series of sessions is conducted by one of the resident Jesuit priests. He is known as the Retreat Master. Following his comments, the silence begins. Participants do not engage in conversation until the completion of the noon mass on Sunday.

There are those who cannot stand the quietness—they go home! For those who cherish the time to be alone with their thoughts, with no TV, telephone, radio, or person to interrupt, it can be a life-changing experience.

The retreat schedule involves a series of lectures provided by the Retreat Master, daily mass, rosary recitation, and a Way of the Cross. No activity is compulsory. Attendees are free to walk the grounds, stay in their room, or participate in the scheduled program. Each meal is a feast for the body and every

182

lecture contains powerful food for the soul. It is an experience like no other I've ever encountered.

Some personal time is allotted for those individuals who may wish to have a private session with a priest. These sessions are an opportunity to talk to someone about any issue that concerns them. These are wonderfully educated and understanding priests who constantly amaze me with their ability to provide sensible and practical solutions to complex issues. Again, this is an option and not a mandatory practice.

For someone who likes to speak as much as I do, I marvel at how much I enjoy the experience of silence. It's life-changing. The time is so precious to me that nothing but death or serious illness of a family member will ever stop me from completing this annual activity.

One final unique thing about the retreat is that there is no requirement to pay. Participants are told what the cost is to cover individual expenses. They are given an unmarked envelope in which to deposit their payment, whatever that is. No one but you and God knows how much you've contributed. Some are very generous. Others give what they can afford. The wonderful thing about this system of payment is that each week more than enough is paid to cover expenses and maintain this beautiful facility.

The power of Manresa's silence gives me an opportunity to bring clarity and focus to my life. Reflecting on the past and how the months ahead can be approached is a much clearer process in the Manresa environment. I have learned how to be a better person and accept the challenges life brings. I have learned how to forgive my weaknesses and grow my strengths. I have learned how to become more tolerable of myself and others. Silence is a powerful stimulator.

If I were to choose a phrase to describe Manresa, I could not say it better than Louis Yarrut does in one of the booklets on Manresa. He described Manresa as *"The house of silence and sacred sod, where nobody speaks to anybody, and everybody speaks to God."*

I've talked about a variety of activities in this book that are all part of building a successful life. I've chosen my closing thoughts about Manresa to demonstrate that true success is a multidimensional process. One must include mental, physical, and spiritual elements to achieve the proper balance. The search is complete when all three are in harmony.

Manresa Prayer

During a recent Manresa retreat, I wrote the following prayer. It's intensely personal but I share it with you in the hope that it will make a difference as you complete your spiritual search. May it bring a powerful message to your soul and peace and tranquillity as you journey through life.

Help me to have an open mind to receive your daily gifts and profit from the experience. Tear down my walls of resistance to your love and let me recognize the ways you are shaping and guiding my life. Help me to use all my talents, and to focus on your love and the goodness and joy of your kingdom.

Thank you for the many blessings you've bestowed upon me, for being there when I needed strength to get through the low moments of my day, for giving me courage to face tomorrow with confidence.

I'm sorry for the times I turned my back on you and fell into the grasp of sin. I ask for your grace to repent and purify my heart so I would eliminate such actions from my life.

I love you and need your love and guidance every moment of my life. I want all my actions to express my love for you. I am deeply grateful for your patience and humbly ask for your forgiveness when I fail to acknowledge how important your love is to me.

Be with me and help me develop the strength to always do your will. Shape my mind to focus on the possibilities of what can be. Be with me so that all my actions are dedicated to fostering your love within me and every person I meet. May I always remain your servant.

Teach me to pray with an open heart so that I can receive your message. Teach me to accept the things I cannot change or control. Give me the courage to act and change the things I can and should. Provide me with the wisdom to know the difference.

I ask these things in your name.   **Amen.**

Three Wishes For You

As you move through your daily activities in your search for success, I want to leave you with three wishes:

My first wish is for you to have the *serenity* to accept the trials and tribulations of life that you cannot change. They will task you, but with serenity, you will prevail.

My second wish is for you to have *courage.* There are things in your life that you can control. They can be changed. Sometimes making those necessary changes will be difficult, but if you persist with courage, you will succeed.

My final wish is for you to possess the *wisdom* to know the difference.

God Bless!
```
```

Action steps
to
success

1. Do you have a "Manresa" experience in your life? If not, what can you do to develop one?

2. Spend time in silent meditation. Begin with a fifteen minute period. Find that spot where you can be totally by yourself with absolutely no distractions. Sit as quietly as you can. Don't even try to think. Just let the silence dominate. When straying thoughts occur, concentrate on your breathing to bring thoughts under control. Continue the practice until you can complete one hour of total silence.

3. By the time you reach this statement, you will have read through the entire book. If I did my part properly, you will have many thoughts on how you can complete your search for success. I would deeply appreciate the opportunity to learn how this book has affected your life.

   As a personal favor, I would appreciate receiving a letter from you acknowledging what you've gained from the time spent reading my words. That information is an important part of my search for success.

Notes & thoughts for action.....

Part X

Lagniappe

██

Reading List

Anderson, Kristin and Ron Zemke. *Delivering Knock Your Socks Off Service.* New York, NY: Amacom, 1991.

Bean, William. *Strategic Planning That Makes Things Happen.* Amherst, MA: HRD Press, Inc., 1993.

Biggs, Dick. *If Life Is A Balancing Act, Why Am I So Darn Clumsy?* Roswell, GA: Chattahoochee Publishers, 1993.

Blanchard, Ken and Don Shula. *Everyone's A Coach.* New York, NY: Harper Business, 1995.

Bristol, Claude M. *The Magic Of Thinking Big.* New York, NY: Cornerstone Library, 1977.

Buechner, Fedrick. *Wishful Thinking.* San Francisco, CA: HarperSanFrancisco, 1993.

Campbell, Ross. *How To Really Love Your Child.* New York, NY: New American Library, 1977.

Canfield, Jack and Mark Victor Hanson. *Chicken Soup For The Soul.* Deerfield, FL: Health Communications, Inc., 1993.

Carnegie, Dale. *How To Win Friends And Influence People.* New York, NY: Pocket Books, 1977.

Carnegie, Dale. *How To Stop Worrying And Start Living.* New York, NY: Pocket Books, 1976.

Charles, C. Leslie. *Stick To It.* East Lansing, MI: Yes! Press, 1995.

Clark-Epstein, Chris. *Simple Encounters.* Wausau, WI: Another Pair of Shoes Press, 1995.

Clauson, George. *The Richest Man In Babylon.* New York, NY: Hawthorn Books, Inc., 1978.

Covy, Stephen R. *The 7 Habits Of Highly Successful People.* New York, NY: Simon and Schuster, 1989.

Covy, Stephen R. *Principle-Centered Leadership.* New York, NY: Summit Books, 1991.

Covy, Stephen R. *First Things First.* New York, NY: Simon and Schuster, 1994.

Curren, Dolores. *Traits Of A Healthy Family.* San Francisco, CA: HarperSanFrancisco, 1983.

Frankl, Viktor E. *Man's Search For Meaning.* New York, NY: Pocket Books, Inc., 1972.

Garfield, Charles. *Peak Performers.* New York, NY: Avon Books, 1987.

Griessman, B. Eugene. *Time Tactics Of Very Successful People.* New York, NY: McGraw-Hill, Inc., 1994.

Hill, Napoleon and W. Clement Stone. *Success Through A Positive Mental Attitude.* New York, NY: Pocket Books, Inc., 1977.

Hill, Napoleon. *Think And Grow Rich.* Hollywood, CA: Wilshire Book Company, 1966.

Jeffries, Elizabeth. *The Heart Of Leadership.* Dubuque, IA: Kendall/Hunt Publishing Company, 1996.

Lakein, Alan. *How To Get Control of Your Time And Your Life.* New York, NY: Signet Book New American Library, 1973.

LeBoeuf, Michael. *Working Smart.* New York, NY: Warner Books, 1979.

LeBoeuf, Michael. *How To Win Customers And Keep Them For Life.* New York, NY: G. P. Putnam, 1988.

LeBoeuf, Michael. *Fast Forward.* New York, NY: G. P. Putnam's Sons, 1993.

Mackenzie, R. Alec. *The Time Trap.* New York, NY: Amacon, 1972.

Maltz, Maxwell. *Psycho-Cybernetics.* New York, NY: Pocket Books, 1977.

Mandino, Og and Buddy Kaye. *The Gift Of Acabar.* New York, NY: Bantam Books, 1979.

Mandino, Og. *The Greatest Miracle In The World.* New York, NY: Bantam Books, 1975.

McGinnis, Alan Loy. *Bringing Out The Best In People.* Minneapolis, MN: Augsburg Publishing House, 1985.

McGinnis, Alan Loy. *The Friendship Factor.* Minneapolis, MN: Augsburg Publishing House, 1979.

Murphy, Joseph. *The Power Of Your Subconscious Mind.* Englewood Cliffs, NJ: Prentice-Hall, Inc., 1978.

Nightingale, Earl. *The Essence Of Success.* Niles, IL: Nightingale-Conant Corporation, 1993.

Olesen, Erik. *12 Steps To Mastering The Winds Of Change.* New York, NY: Macmillan Publishing Company, 1993.

Peale, Norman Vincent. *The Power Of Positive Thinking.* New York, NY: Fawcett Crest, 1956.

Peck, M. Scott. *The Road Less Traveled.* New York, NY: Simon and Schuster, 1978.

Powell, John and Loretta Brady. *Will The Real Me Please Stand Up?* Allen, TX: Tabor Publishing, 1985.

Powell, John. *Why Am I Afraid To Tell You Who I Am?* Allen, TX: Tabor Publishing, 1969.

Powell, John. *Happiness Is An Inside Job.* Allen, TX: Tabor Publishing, 1989.

Rich, Dorothy. *MegaSkills.* Boston, MA: Houghton Mifflin Co., 1988.

Schwartz, David. *The Magic Of Thinking Big.* Hollywood, CA: Wilshire Book Company, 1978.

Spera Rosenfeld, Jo Ann. *Yeah, You Rite!* New Orleans, LA: Medica-Spera, Inc., 1995.

Smith, Hyrum. *The 10 Natural Laws Of Successful Time And Life Management.* New York, NY: Warner Books, 1994.

Stone, W. Clement. *The Success System That Never Fails.* New York, NY: Pocket Books, 1980.

Tweed, Stephen. *Strategic Focus.* Hollywood, FL: Fell Publishers, Inc., 1990.

Waitley, Denis. *Seeds Of Greatness.* New York, NY: Pocket Books, 1984.

Waitley, Denis. *The Joy Of Working.* New York, NY: Ballantine Books, 1986.

Wall, Bob, Robert Solum and Mark Sobol. *The Visionary Leader.* Rocklin, CA: Prima Publishing, 1992.

Ziglar, Zig. *See You At The Top.* Gretna, LA: Pelican Publishing Company, 1978.

About the author

Billy Arcement, M.Ed., is a professional speaker, author, and consultant. He has spoken to audiences from Beijing, China to Baton Rouge, Louisiana. He brings to the platform a wealth of knowledge on management and leadership skills, quality systems, and personal and organizational strategic planning. His years of study of success principles provide audiences with a thorough mastery of what it takes to build a successful life and an effective organization.

A former teacher and coach, he also has twenty-seven years experience in the business sector, with twenty-three in a management capacity.

Billy was a twelve-year member of his local school board and is a past president of his board and the Louisiana School Boards Association. He is only the second person in LSBA history to serve two years as state president.

He is a member of the National Speakers Association and a past president of the New Orleans Chapter. He has written nationally published articles on education, management, and success principles.

His clients come from business, education, government, and associations. A trademark of his talks is a highly customized format specifically designed for client needs. He offers practical solutions and helps his audiences **turn knowledge into results!**

Programs that produce results include:

School Board Performance That Makes A Difference

This title covers a variety of highly customized programs offered to school boards. **School board retreats** emphasize in-depth review of individual board performance, teambuilding skills, strategic planning initiatives, and problem solving skills.

School board association conference programs include keynotes, preconvention workshops, and break-out sessions on a variety of subjects such as board evaluation, teambuilding and leadership skills and change.

How To Create A Winning Quality Team

Designed in modular format, this series of programs covers the quality process from implementation to employee empowerment.

How To Master Your Time And Your Life

This seminar covers the essential elements of an effective time and life management system and strategies for goal achievement.

It's Attitude, Not Aptitude, That Gives You Altitude

Participants are shown how to develop, control, maintain, and use positive attitudes to build a successful life. This is the number one lesson most people never learn.

People Are Your Most Important Business

A common sense approach to managing people. It covers human relations, leadership, motivation, and communication skills. A very popular people-oriented management seminar.

Three Keys For Building Success In Your Business And Personal Life

A simple yet powerful formula that covers the basics upon which EVERY success is built. It is a down-to-earth approach to successful living.

Keynotes can be developed from some of the above topics. There are also a variety of other motivational and inspirational messages offered that are just right for your audience.

All programs carry an unconditional 100% guarantee.

For information on Billy Arcements' speeches, seminars, consulting services, newsletter, *Lagniappe,* and book orders, please contact him at:

Results Press
Billy Arcement
108 South Magnolia Drive
Donaldsonville, LA 70346
(504) 473-4346